LUKE'S STORY OF PAUL

Richard I. Pervo

FORTRESS PRESS   MINNEAPOLIS

Related
Fortress Press Titles

Matthew's Story of Jesus
by Richard Edwards

Mark's Story of Jesus
by Werner Kelber

Luke's Story of Jesus
by O. C. Edwards

John's Story of Jesus
by Robert Kysar

LUKE'S STORY OF PAUL

Scripture quotations, unless otherwise noted, are from the Revised Standard Version of the Bible, copyright © 1946, 1952, and 1971 by the Division of Christian Education of the National Council of Churches.

Library of Congress Cataloging-in-Publication Data

Pervo, Richard I.
    Luke's story of Paul / Richard I. Pervo.
      p. cm.
    ISBN 0-8006-2405-X
    1. Bible. N.T. Acts—Criticism, interpretation, etc. 2. Paul,
the Apostle, Saint. I. Title.
BS2625.2.P38   1990
226'.606—dc20   89-27342
                                         CIP

The paper used in this publication meets the minimum requirements of American National Standard for Information Sciences—Permanence of Paper for Printed Library Materials, ANSI Z329.48-1984. ∞™

Manufactured in the U.S.A.   AF 1-2405

94   93   92   91   2   3   4   5   6   7   8   9   10

Iohannis A. Hollar

R.I.P.

Ad perennis vitae fontem mens sitit nunc arida,
Claustra carnis praesto frangi clausa quaerit anima,
Gliscit, ambit, eluctatur exul frui patria.

St. Peter Damian

Vitaque cum gemitu fugit indignata sub umbris

Vergil

Contents

Preface

This book intends to be a sequel to *Luke's Story of Jesus* (Fortress Press, 1981), by my colleague at Seabury-Western, O. C. Edwards, Jr. I am most grateful to him for assistance and support rendered over many years.

The nontechnical nature of this work deprives me of the opportunity to acknowledge my frequent dependence upon other authors. Those who seek a rationale for the literary understanding of Acts presented in the following pages may consult my *Profit with Delight: The Literary Genre of the Acts of the Apostles* (Fortress Press, 1987).

This book is dedicated to the members and friends of the Church of the Transfiguration, Pointe Aux Pins, Michigan.

Introduction

The work of the author called "Luke" constitutes the largest contribution by a single writer to the New Testament—and some of its most perplexing treasures and richest puzzles. What motivated an early Christian not only to supersede the Gospel of Mark, but also to continue the story? Is Luke-Acts *two* stories or a single work divided by the requirements of ancient book production? Answers to these questions vary.

Contemporary scholarship tends to stress the unity of Luke and Acts (whence "Luke-Acts"). The merits of this emphasis are obvious. The preface to each work implies a unity, an implication undergirded by numerous structural parallels and cross-references. The most vigorous assertion of the unity of Luke-Acts regards their separation as a canonical accident—or error—requiring correction if adequate understanding is to be sought. Since current biblical scholars emphasize the text itself, rather than sources, parallels, or constituent forms, advocacy of the unity of Luke-Acts is the dominant trend.

Historically the two books have enjoyed different and largely separate fates. Luke has been studied in relation to the other Gospels, Matthew and Mark in particular, and with the methods applied to them. In the course of the past century the evangelists have come to be seen as theologians first and foremost, proclaimers of a message rather than narrators of a life. In the case of Acts, however, matters have been different. There comparison has centered upon the epistles of Paul, for which Acts seems to provide a historical frame. Acts has thus been enmeshed in a network of historical and theological controversies regarding its historical value and its representation of the theology of Paul and others. Unlike the Gospels, Acts has not often been permitted to stand upon its own right as an independent literary production. Proponents of a unified treatment of Luke-Acts seek to rectify this neglect.

If Luke-Acts is to be viewed as a self-contained and distinct unity, what kind of writing is it? When Luke was evaluated in the context of the other Gospels, this problem was not acute, for the presence of four distinct Gospels offers some notion of what a gospel is. The inclusion of Acts raises two questions. With what is Acts itself to be compared? Is it history, biography, or a unique creation of its author? The differences between Luke and Acts make it difficult to assign them to the same genre without further ado. Thus scholars do not agree whether these differences require viewing Luke and Acts as two variations of a single literary type, two books containing two literary genres, or a single (and singular) kind of writing. By composing a book on Acts alone, I reveal that I understand each to represent a particular literary type.

The problem of the literary genre of Acts is not, however, the subject of this work. My purpose is to help readers appreciate Acts as a sequel to the Gospel of Luke, without reference to the Pauline epistles, early church history, or the sources employed; and without supplementing, correcting, or defending its text. All these activities are supremely important, to be sure, but both scholarly and liturgical uses of Scripture tend to fragment the text and focus upon its periphery. Recent criticism has witnessed a healthy reaction against the dominance of such fragmentation, stressing instead the uniqueness and integrity of each document and the structures and purposes of the writings themselves. This is one presupposition underlying my attempt to present the story of Acts.

Another is the renewed appreciation of our day for storytelling as a medium of theological discourse. We express who we are and what we value by telling our stories, for we are actors in the midst of a story rather than points upon a spectrum or abstractions derived from books. Our stories are inevitably enmeshed with the stories of other persons and groups. Christians have been nurtured by Bible stories, especially the Gospels, that explicate the creed by telling the story of Jesus. Of all the evangelists it is Luke who uses the medium of the story most effectively to explain the origin and identity of the Christian community he addressed. Luke is thus most deserving of having his story told. "Story" is here understood as something more than a frame or shell to be discarded in the quest for underlying substance, but in and of itself as a factor of communication that shapes understanding. If any New Testament writer is a narrative theologian, it is Luke.

Luke is an artist and theologian who communicates by telling stories. Because the Gospels and Acts present a coherent story with a narrative plot, they may be studied with techniques developed in the study of other narrative works shaped by plot structures—that is, novels. This angle of approach presumes that they are imaginative creations. Some will, of course, find such an approach irreverent, or worse. This method need not, however, reduce the sacred books to the level of fiction, concoctions of their authors (if that is, in fact, reduction). For us human interpreters it may matter little whether one assigns inspiration to the Holy Spirit or to the literary genius of the author. It is difficult to contend that inspired authors should have less creativity, imagination, or art than noninspired writers.

Those who regard stories, including biblical stories, as providing direct access to events do themselves and the stories a disservice. Stories about real or imagined events select, focus, channel, and control the interpretations they and we make. Through our understandings we have opportunity to participate in and create the events of our own individual and collective understandings. Modern literary criticism reflects upon the world created by the act of reading literature, the narrative world brought into being by books, and regards the act of reading itself as a creative and imaginative process. Everyone who has read a book and then seen the movie will grasp the essential point of this critical endeavor. These reflections have great importance for religions that possess as one of their major marks a collection of sacred writings. Christianity is one such religion.

Sacred writings presuppose what is called a "symbolic universe," the patterns by which people arrange, interpret, and evaluate the data with which they are bombarded. The understanding of a book requires recognition of its symbolic universe rather than the imposition of another. Since writers like Luke do not fully clarify their symbolic universes through such media as "prefaces," readers must discover it for themselves. That is part of the enjoyment of reading.

It is toward the world created by the narrative of Acts and the symbolic universe depicted therein that my attention is directed, a world regarded as vibrant and real independently of its links to the "real world" it reflects. I believe that those who can read Luke's story with only skepticism or defensiveness will spoil its fun. Acts is a book meant, among other things, to be enjoyed. The reader of this book who experiences that enjoyment will have fulfilled my expectations.

Explanation is one means for enhancing appreciation. In addition to explanation I shall often seek to illuminate the magic of Luke's narrative art through evocation, attempting rather to respond to the literary power of Acts than merely in every instance to describe it. Instead of listing various Lukan techniques in this introduction, I shall usually identify them as they emerge, noting some other instances and attempting to leave room for further discoveries by the reader. There are three exceptions to this method.

One of the principal pleasures in reading Luke-Acts is the discovery of its interconnectedness, the "parallels" large and small, and the cross-references within the text. Some of these become visible in the discovery of the general architecture of each book and of both together. Not all are restricted to this general framework. Luke sprinkles his work with hints and allusions pointing forward and backward, providing a nearly inexhaustible treasure of links by which the various components illuminate one another. Some of these are readily apparent. Others are much more subtle and may rely upon particular Greek words. Many will be noted in parentheses, and those who pursue them will find fruitful stimulation. Most will not be noted, for, once again, I hope to encourage frequent rereadings and personal discovery of the myriad threads with which Luke has woven his marvelous tapestry.

Luke is the type of narrator called "reliable." When, for example, he says that Cornelius was a "devout man who feared God with all his household, gave alms liberally to the people, and prayed constantly to God" (Acts 10:2), we know that this is so, that the statement is not an ironic introduction to the portrayal of a hypocrite. Luke does, however, admit characters who will deliver unreliable information in speeches. People will lie.

As a narrator Luke is also omniscient. He can bring the readers into closed meetings and allow them to overhear private conversations, read letters, and even peer into individual minds. The gift of omniscience permits the narrator to escort readers to every desired place, there to see and hear all that is required.

One of Luke's primary artistic gifts is the capacity to spring imagination by a word or a phrase rather than by elaborate or protracted exposition. Through this economy the author can suggest an entire scene or circumstance with a few words. My exposition will often attempt to bring forth some of the implications resident in these brief sketches. These evocations do not, of course, seek to be normative, for by this paucity of circumstantial detail Luke allows and invites readers to create their own scenes and fill in incidents. The creations of individual readers will naturally differ.

In addition to the obligation of aiding readers to grasp the work as a whole, I have a further, almost contrary, goal: to attempt to present the story in its freshness and assist each reader to approach Acts with the naiveté of a "first reader," one who does not know how the story will turn out. The attempts to keep these two balls in the air will sometimes lead to dropping one or both.

My working hypotheses about Acts are that it was written by the author of the Gospel of Luke, who was unlikely to have been a companion of Paul, but a writer of the third Christian generation. The text of Acts suggests that the work was directed to Christians in the region around the Aegean Sea, perhaps Ephesus, probably at the end of the first century. Within the community addressed are some rich persons as well as many poor. Controversies exist about the nature and style of leadership, and divergent understandings of the message—"heresies"—have created conflict. There are also questions about the relation of the church to the world, a subject about which Luke is rather optimistic. But by far the most vexing question is that of the relation of church to synagogue, of emergent

Christianity to the Judaism that arose following the destruction of the temple (A.D. 70). Jews and Christians have gone their separate ways, but the roots they share make this division bitter. Paul and the legitimacy of the missionary communities he established are the focal point of this controversy and the focal point of Acts.

Luke portrays Jews and gentiles who believe in Christ as the true Israel, heirs to the ancient promises. Toward unbelieving Jews he is not always charitable, and some of his characterizations create problems for one who would tell the story of Acts without intervention. Judaism and Christianity have long had their distinct histories, poisoned by more than fifteen hundred years of persecution and the horror of the Holocaust. The nature of Jewish-Christian tensions has changed considerably, a fact readers of Acts have not always appreciated. In retelling them in Lukan terms I must often rely upon the reader's discretion and maturity.

1
An End and a Beginning

1:1—2:42

A NEW DEPARTURE (1:1-14)

Acts opens with the departure of the risen Lord, the selection of a twelfth apostle, and the arrival of the promised Spirit, followed by a period of remarkable life and growth unmarred by conflict or opposition.

Because ancient books essentially lacked such convenient devices as titles for chapters, paragraphing, different typefaces, and the numerous other means by which modern readers are guided through transitions, their authors had to place such information within the text. This was true also of "prefaces," when used. These enclosed prefaces, not unlike many prefaces of today, often followed quite conventional lines. The preface to Acts indicates the beginning of a new book and refers readers to the original preface (Luke 1:1-4), which should be read.

Dedications, likewise, were incorporated. Luke-Acts has a dedicatee, "the most excellent Theophilus." If a real person is intended, he is unknown. The address suggests an individual of high standing, a type Luke would like to attract and whose viewpoint he often represents. One could choose to read the name as symbolic (it means "friend of God"). Theophilus would then be the "ideal reader" Luke has in mind, an individual instructed in the faith and a believer, for those lacking information about Christianity would find Luke and Acts incomprehensible. This reader is aware of other accounts and prepared for one that is more "orderly" and complete.

Secondary prefaces, like those of Acts (1:1-2), normally summarized the previous book and previewed the present volume. Luke prefers instead to place this forecast on the lips of Jesus (1:8), revealing his preference for the use of direct speech. Indeed, the book leaps from the preface directly into the action, sweeping the reader from distant observation into participation. The beginning of this new story overlaps, and conflicts, with the ending of Luke, which seems in every way final and apparently reports the ascension. Only upon coming to Acts does the reader learn of the forty-day period of instruction after Easter. This span conforms to the length of Moses' sojourn with God and neatly rounds off the story of the ministry of Jesus on earth, which was preceded by forty days in the wilderness. By 1:2 the apostles are already in the fore, where they shall long remain. Through these means Luke depicts the continuity of the faith throughout history. By his leap into the words of the risen Lord he indicates the commitment to vividness that will color his story.

The setting of this apostolic instruction, like that of the church, and often of Jesus' teaching in the Gospel, is at table. In the course of this meal Jesus specifies the promise of Luke 24:49 as the gift of the Spirit. Rather than await the establishment of a messianic kingdom on earth, the apostles are directed away from Jerusalem. The ends of the earth, not the end of the world, is the subject of this story.

Working like a film director, Luke has cut directly into a gradually unfolding scene. Only in v. 12 do readers discover that they have been listening to a farewell address on the Mount of Olives. We observe the ascension from the viewpoint of the apostles. Interpreting angels clarify the meaning of this event and, like the two at the tomb (Luke 24:4-5), challenge the onlookers with a question. By this structural similarity Luke conveys the paschal character of the ascension. It is an Easter event, not an appendix to the resurrection. The angels also deliver a promise that Jesus will return in glory. Those who believe this promise will not sit about in idle expectation. So closes the period of Easter appearances, ending one era and foreshadowing both the ultimate coming of Christ and the imminent arrival of the empowering Spirit.

The prosaic geographical reference in 1:12 returns our feet firmly to the ground. Luke then takes inventory of the personnel. Lists of names in Acts precede important events. The roster of the apostles is that of Luke 6:13-16, guaranteeing the authenticity of the tradition. There are also changes. Only eleven apostles remain, among whom John has advanced in place to reflect a changed status. Most importantly, Jesus' women disciples are given explicit recognition, together with members of Jesus' family. The former group portrays inclusiveness, the latter changes in leadership. Luke frequently operates in this way, introducing change by depiction rather than description. Readers may either regard them as "natural" and read on undisturbed, or view such subtle devices as invitations to read with greater attention. Like the house churches of Luke's own day, the "primitive" group assembles for worship in the upper room of an urban building (cf. 20:8).

EQUIPMENT FOR MINISTRY (1:15-26)

The next scene recounts the selection of a twelfth apostle. Peter's changed role is portrayed rather than explained. The new mode for interpreting Scripture proclaimed in Luke 24 becomes apparent. For the first time also the presence of Divine Providence to guide the community manifests itself. While defining the office of apostle in such a way as to create a bridge between the earthly and heavenly ministries of Jesus, Peter introduces concepts relevant to church leadership in Luke's day, as reflected by the terms *episkopē* and *diakonia*, and, in particular, the theme of money. For the first time also the reader is led to reflect on the condign punishments meted out from on high upon sinners. All this information comes through the medium of a speech. When Peter recalls the wretched fate of perfidious Judas and provides the translation of an Aramaic word (*Akeldama*), he does so for the benefit of the readers. In the speeches of Acts Luke communicates with readers. The reference to lots (note the Greek wordplay in vv. 17 and 26) sharply distinguishes the present situation from the period when the Spirit will make such choices (as in 13:1-3) and establishes a thematic link to the opening of Luke (1:9). In this, the first of several church meetings depicted in Acts, it is clear that the community is no mad sect, but a dignified body that conducts its affairs like a civic assembly.

THE PROMISED GIFT (2:1-13)

Then comes the day of Pentecost, a Jewish feast. This occasion will give opportunity for the presence of a festive crowd and exhibit the continuity of salvation history. Luke presents the gift of the Spirit by telling a story, a story that does not limit the event but proclaims its meaning, a meaning made even more apparent in the subsequent sermon, baptisms, and miraculous community life. Peter's sermon shows that events require interpretation. By themselves the events are ambiguous (cf. 2:13).

Assembled for prayer, the community experiences a sudden onrush of signs resembling a classic Old Testament epiphany: sound, wind, thunder. (The cloud of 1:9 and earthquake of 4:31 complete the list and thus enclose this entire portion of Acts within the frame of an epiphany.) With dizzying speed the gust of apparent wind brings fiery tongues resting upon each individual. The gift of the spirit is a gift of speech. John's promise is fulfilled in a way reminiscent of the baptism of Jesus (Luke 3:21-22). Through these arresting images Luke seizes our imagination and expresses the origin and nature of the gift. The primitive power of these images also evokes the story of creation. New creation is the subject here.

With equal suddenness the scene shifts and the house dissolves. Devout Jewish residents of and visitors to Jerusalem appear, astonished at the "voice" (cf. Luke 3:23). The following scene brilliantly foreshadows the course of the book in an atmosphere of intense excitement, as representatives of "the ends of the earth" miraculously hear the message addressing them in their native tongues. The wind here roaring will not cease until its mighty blast blows Paul to Rome. If the miracle is one of speech, the gift takes the form of hearing. Through this classic tale Luke portrays the power of new creation to shatter barriers and restore the unity of the human race (cf. also 17:16-34).

THE PROMISE OFFERED (2:14-42)

This is, however, a cosmopolitan crowd, no less sophisticated than the Athenians (compare 2:13 to 17:18). Wonder rubs shoulders with doubt. Peter steps in to clarify the situation with a compelling sermon. Jesus also had preached an inaugural sermon following his empowerment by the Spirit (Luke 4:16-30). Flanked by an impressive entourage of colleagues, the apostle opens with an oratorical appeal, brushing away the allegation of drunkenness and explaining the events as fulfillment of the prophecy of Joel, which is cited in detail (2:14-21) to demonstrate that the present is the time of fulfillment. To the national groups represented in the catalogue of nations the citation adds old and young, male and female, increasing the universal scope of this gift. Unlike Matthew, for example, who would tell a story and comment "this took place in order to fulfill . . . ," Luke achieves this end without injecting his own voice.

The second section of Peter's sermon reveals careful construction, with opening and closing credal statements framing the central proclamation of the resurrection, which, in turn, is buttressed on either side by scriptural quotations. It sets forth basic Lukan theological understandings. Jesus, whose wondrous deeds demonstrated divine authorization, died in accordance with God's plan, at the hands of sinners, and was subsequently exalted and empowered to bestow the Spirit. The apostles are his witnesses. For Luke the "earthly" Jesus is a great prophet like Moses, Elijah, and Elisha, killed like other prophets by his own people. His death is not presented as a saving event. This is a popular theology, rational, and premised by the scheme of promise and fulfillment.

Dialogue enlivens the close of Peter's sermon. The crowd, cut to the quick, raises the basic question of potential converts and receives a straightforward answer (cf. Luke 3:10-14). Luke's subsequent summary suggests a protracted appeal that met with considerable success. Three thousand converts is not a bad day's work for a community that saw the sun rise with one hundred twenty members on its rolls. This kind of casual mention of a tremendous number at the end is a technique of miracle stories. In this instance it testifies to the miraculous explosion of new life.

LIFE IN THE SPIRIT (1) (2:43-47)

The concluding summary gives further explication of the gift of new life. Baptism leads to life together, sharing of property no less than worship. Like the gift of tongues, this wonder is utopian in that it restores the primitive condition of the human race, undivided by national or personal boundaries. The similarity of this description to our worship (instruction, prayer, offering, Eucharist) pierces our hearts with the recognition that worship is not an escape from life but a model for it. The crescendo of joy accompanied by numerical increase presents Luke's understanding of spiritual growth. This summary is a paradigmatic description of the ground and warrant for the existence of the community. The shot that will be heard around the world has been fired. It is a logical, God-given consequence of Easter. There are no clouds of opposition on the horizon, and the notion of including gentiles receives but a faint hint (2:39). How will the community under its leaders react to external hostility and internal dissent? Read on.

2

The Wages of Repression

3:1—8:3

The comfortable situation of the early days gives way to a rising tide of opposition, directed first at the leaders and ultimately against the entire community. In the face of increasing hostility and persecution, the community continues to prosper and grow. New members bring internal problems, but these too are readily corrected. Repression in Acts leads always to mission.

Into the placid pool of life together, the rock of opposition falls, producing ripples that become waves culminating in the ferocious vortex of stones that overwhelmed Stephen. The counterpoint line depicts community life in which incipient problems are nipped in the bud before they inhibit growth of the organism. In chaps. 3–7 Luke makes threefold use of a pattern, consisting of miracle, which draws attention and followers, teaching to those attracted, the subsequent arrest of one or more leaders, a trial, and, finally, miraculous vindication. Variation in detail prevents any impression of monotony, and each of the three cycles exhibits an intensification of repression. In chaps. 3 and 4 Peter and John are targets, followed by all the apostles in chap. 5, and the seven in chaps. 6–7, climaxing with a general persecution in 8:1. With each incident tension mounts.

We witness the gradual slide of the Sanhedrin down the scale of justice. Varied marvels color the account and contrast with official obstinance. Through this exciting report Luke establishes a case against the recalcitrant leaders and people of Jerusalem. The ignorance that may have excused them for Jesus' death hardens into blindness. At the same time the seedbed of the gentile mission is being prepared. Its sowing will not shock the reader. To all this Luke adds a selection of thrilling speeches.

GIVING RATHER THAN RECEIVING (3:1-26)

As noted in 2:46, the temple remains at the center of community worship. Peter and John are on their accustomed way to prayer. The scene opens, however, with the appearance of a cripple, no hysteric, but a lifelong victim of disability also on his way to the temple. He must be transported by friends to practice the only profession open to him, beggary. The temple provided an opportunity for those devoted to prayer to add almsgiving to their virtues (cf. 10:1-2), so there his friends bore the poor cripple. Peter and John arrive, and we do not doubt that such pious leaders of a sharing community will give what they have. They do, although the gift surpasses expectations. The dramatically effective reference to money informs the readers that the apostles do not have community funds at their personal disposal. Healers with money in their pockets are liable to be magicians. What they do have to give is a cure. Like Jesus, the apostles can heal. Their formula uses the Lord's name, introducing the leitmotif of this chapter. Peter raised the former cripple, symbolizing his rise to new life, just as the reference to his mother's womb (v. 2) had symbolized the old creation. He acts out this new life with ecstatic praise to God. The wording of 3:8 recalls Isa. 35:6, the fulfillment of which Jesus had proclaimed in Luke 7:22. In his name that fulfillment continues. What could be a more appropriate place for this act than the temple, center of worship and abode of God's name?

The same temple was the focal point of Luke 1–2. The new story recapitulates the old. Jesus taught in the temple, and his apostles will do likewise, as they move from the gate to the portico of Solomon where, in the manner of ancient philosophers, Peter and John confront a throng of rapt onlookers. As in chap. 2, miracle serves as the bait to attract a crowd. The stage is set for a second sermon of Peter, who will interpret the event.

Like the previous sermon, this speech is well constructed. Its content is similar, but here the name of Jesus and his various titles occupy a central place, and the invitation to repentance is fuller. The people of Jerusalem are responsible for Jesus' death, ironically condemning the author of life, but their repentance will bring forgiveness and "times of refreshment," a foretaste of which the former beggar has enjoyed (3:19-21; cf. 1:6-8). Abraham's name comes as a reminder that the promises of God encompass all (v. 25). This is a subject Acts will take up again.

IN DEFENSE OF GIVING (4:1-22)

Just as Peter has rounded off his sermon with a return to the message of the resurrection and an appeal to relinquish evil, the forces of evil irrupt upon them (as they had upon Jesus [Luke 22:47]), in the persons of an arresting party composed of priests, the head of the temple constabulary, and Sadducees. These last regard the apostles' teaching as usurpation and resent their proclamation of resurrection, especially in connection with agitation about Jesus. Because it is too late in the day for a trial, the prisoners must spend the night in durance vile while readers wait in suspense. Luke punctuates the episode with a statistical summary: five thousand men were fed to satisfaction with the message.

With the coming of day the pair are arraigned before the Sanhedrin. On this, its first, appearance in Acts that body is portrayed in all its solemnity and power. Against such authority and prestige, what can two humble Galileans do? The Sanhedrin does not dispute the fact of the healing, but its authorization. Similar challenges had been raised about the basis for Jesus' teaching and healing (Luke 11:14, 20:2). The Sanhedrin wishes to convict them of practicing magic. Peter crushes this charge before it can get off the ground, politely but deftly inquiring whether they are under indictment for benefaction. Such *euergesia*, "benefaction," was the privilege and prerogative of the wealthy and powerful, of members of the Sanhedrin, for example. Luke 22:25 echoes here. Moving then to the question posed, Peter sets forth the same creed proclaimed to the crowd, albeit with contrasting result.

The elegance of these yokels takes the pillars of their community aback. In the contretemps between two ex-fishermen lacking professional education or social credentials and the Sanhedrin the power of Pentecost is manifest. Jesus had forecast this in Luke 21:15. Now it is the Sanhedrin that finds itself in hot water. Having ineptly included the former beggar in their inquiry, its members had presented Peter and John with a visible model of Jesus' power. Lest their embarrassment become known, they have the accused taken away, then ruminate about their options. We readers can remain in the room and hear them pose this question: "What shall we do?" Peter's first hearers had raised the same query in response to an apostolic address (2:37). Here the motive differs. Unable to cover up the wonder, the Sanhedrin plan to limit the damage by issuing a gag order, apparently confident in their authority.

This confidence was misplaced, and even their futile effort to lock the barn door after the horse has escaped backfires. Peter and John assume the classic pose of philosophers withstanding tyrants. Each side has revealed its colors. The witless Sanhedrin can do no more than utter threats, restrained from more drastic action by popular sentiment. Like Jesus, the apostles work healings and teach in the temple. Like him, they receive popular admiration and official disapproval. Knowing the outcome of Jesus' confrontation with these authorities, readers feel growing trepidation. The issue is clearly drawn. On the one side stand the commandments of God, on the other human opinion.

SHAKING THE WORLD (4:23-31)

Following the return of Peter and John, the community offers an inspired, unison prayer, addressed to the true ruler of the universe. Their words are an example of early Christian theological activity. Prayerful reflection upon Scripture reveals the meaning of events. Psalm 2 foretells the death of Jesus through gentile and Jewish collaboration. Implicit within this exegesis and reflection is the conviction that disciples share the master's fate. Peter and John are experiencing the rejection Jesus faced. They therefore do not pray for rescue, but for courage. Heaven ratifies their petitions with an earthquake, and earth shows forth its answer in their continued bold proclamation. Key words ("threats," "boldness," "healing," "name") make this scene an integral part of the previous proceedings. The gospel has rocked the Sanhedrin and will shake the world.

LIFE IN THE SPIRIT (2) (4:32—5:16)

Following this impressive testimony to the power of prayer are two stories about community life, enclosed between two summaries (4:32-37; 5:12-16). The community was of one heart, and where its heart is, there its treasure will also be (Luke 6:45). An earlier summary whetted our appetites with a description of community life (2:42-47), characterized by *koinōnia* (fellowship, sharing, communion). Now comes a fuller description, to demonstrate that opposition has not deflected the community from the narrow path and to provide some relief from the stories of persecution and danger.

The remarkable capacity for unison prayer (4:24) is crowned with the even more remarkable capacity for unison property. Believers have achieved an ancient political dream and philosophical ideal by holding all in common. Deuteronomy 15:4 reveals that this also satisfied a biblical imperative. Holders of real property were willing to liquidate their estates and place the proceeds into a common fund administered by the apostles. Wealthy residents of Greco-Roman cities gave large sums of money for the public good, but they determined its use and were hailed as benefactors. In the Christian community donors lost their power over their money and most of the honor. (Unless there is some bond between sharing resurrection witness and sharing material goods, 4:33 is an intrusion into the summary.)

Two exemplary case histories reinforce the general exposition. Barnabas enters the story by giving up his property. The full introduction suggests that he may have an important role to play. The nickname suggests preaching ability (13:15; Heb. 13:22). As a Levite he represents authentic Judaism. As a Cypriot he introduces the Diaspora. Each of these factors will enter into the story.

The tale of Ananias and Sapphira begins with promise. They, too, liquidated property, but desired to bask in the aura of sacrifice while holding back some of their proceeds. This did not work. Peter knew that they were pretending that they had given their all. The source of such deception is Satan (as in Luke 22:3, where Judas also received money). The contrast drawn between God and mortals (5:4) links this incident to the preceding encounter with the Sanhedrin. When Peter had finished his denunciation, Ananias fell dead. The like fate of his wife eliminates any possibility that his demise was coincidental. No sooner has she demonstrated her guilt than her burial party bursts upon the scene. The couple who had claimed to deposit their wealth at the feet of Peter were themselves soon deposited six feet under. What they had given up may have been as difficult for them as the passage through the eye of a needle, but it did not get them into the kingdom of heaven. Their dire fate is a reminder that Satan is not restricted to the realm of wicked priests and officials. Those who know their Bible will recall the story of Achan (Joshua 7), during the early days in the promised land.

Acts 5:12-16 reveals that the events of chap. 3 were but illustrations of an extensive list of miracles and missions. Despite the warnings issued by the Sanhedrin, healings abound, and the portico of Solomon becomes a regular preaching station. Numbers grow. The suburbs are penetrated. Demons flee. As even Peter's shadow conveys healing power, the authorities sit in the lengthening shadow of darkness and gloom. How long will they sit still for this?

WHO IS IN CHARGE? (5:17-42)

Not very long. Lashing out in rage, the jealous authorities, dominated by the resurrection-denying Sadducees, clap their hands upon the twelve and fling them into jail. The next day (4:1) will bring a trial, and there is no reason to suspect that the accused will be pampered. Imagining that they have safely contained this pernicious gospel, the Sadducees can slumber with visions of vengeance dancing in their heads. While they dream, an angel is foiling their plans by freeing the apostles, not so that they may escape, but so that their work may go on. Without a thought for the work of angels (in whom they do not believe, 23:8), the authorities assemble in all their constitutional splendor and juridical dignity to eradicate once and for all this noxious menace. When the menials dispatched to drag in the accused return, the Sanhedrin discovers that there has been a hitch in the proceedings: the (carefully secured) prisoners are not available! This report throws the stately chamber into unseemly confusion, confusion scarcely relieved by the opportune arrival of a messenger to advise them of what the reader already knows. Guards are then dispatched to extricate the unrepentant band from the temple. So popular are the twelve that the deed will require some finesse, lest the crowd prevent the arrest with stones. This is not the last we shall hear of stones, but at present the officials are separated from their constituency by a chasm of potential violence.

The difficult arrest takes place without a hitch, allowing the trial to go ahead as planned. The chief priest rather lamely repeats the earlier warning, together with a bit of whining about the attempt to blame the Sanhedrin for Jesus' execution. Led by Peter, the twelve staunchly reassert the need to obey God rather than mortals. Having implied that heaven has not sanctioned these august proceedings, Peter continues with a summary of the creed that does, indeed, indict the Sanhedrin for Jesus' death.

In their resultant fury the judges resolve to put the apostles to death, a resolution that would doubtless have been carried out had not a learned and venerable Pharisee named Gamaliel been able to obtain recognition. After requesting that the prisoners be briefly excused, Gamaliel offers a few remarks, the burden of which, supported by two examples of the fate in store for terrorist movements, fundamentally confirms the thesis of Peter. What God supports cannot be vanquished, and those who attempt the same will be guilty of blasphemy. What God does not favor will be crushed. This wisdom saved the apostles, although the officials gave the divine will a nudge by reiterating their now stale warnings, driven home with a whipping. Utterly undaunted, the apostles rejoice in sharing their Lord's apparent disgrace and return to their ministry in temple and home.

And now, dear reader, please extract yourself for a moment from this story and observe what Luke has accomplished within the compass of twenty-five verses: a frightening arrest, a marvelous delivery, a thrilling trial, and suspense galore. Two concise speeches enliven the narrative. Despite the escalation of real and potential violence, witness goes consistently on. Gamaliel's speech is a little gem. Through the mouth of a prominent member of the high council Luke displays the enormous gap between followers of Jesus and advocates of military resistance. The great Pharisee can say, "Wait and see what comes of this." We who know of the angelic intervention, to mention but one incident, know full well what will come. We shall not have to wait to see where God is in all this, but how the council will respond, what its members will be prepared to acknowledge, and just how long they might wait.

NEW OCCASIONS TEACH NEW DUTIES (6:1-7)

As the lines between apostles and Sanhedrin harden, other transitions come to light. Acts 5:42 is the last reference to teaching in the temple. Focus now moves toward the synagogue. As the community expands, it reaches Greek-speaking Jews (like Barnabas). Ethnic conflict arises when their "widows" (for Luke's first readers this meant a group with some features of a religious order) complain that they are being shortchanged in the charitable distribution. In words reminiscent of Num. 11:4-26 and Exod. 18:7-13, the Twelve issue a call for additional leaders to provide a twofold ministry of leadership and service. Seven are selected and qualified by prayer and the imposition of hands. Lists of names presage major changes (cf. 1:13, 13:1-3, 20:4). This list begins with Stephen, whose gifts receive emphasis, followed by Philip. At the end is Nicholas, born a gentile and from Antioch. The significance of these data will become clear in due time.

THE DEATH OF AN EXPERT WITNESS (6:8—8:3)

The notes on growth bracketing the previous unit (6:1-7) suggest that the problem arose because of growth and, once solved, led to further growth. In this episode Luke introduces a new group, Greek-speaking Jews, and new personalities. Those who wish to read of the challenges faced by Stephen in managing the community welfare program and mediating between groups of widows will be disappointed. Stephen rather does just what the apostles have been doing, complete with miracles and incontrovertible sermons. The arena of this ministry is the synagogue; its audience, Diaspora Jews. In general, his message is not welcome there. This target will remain in focus for the rest of the book, with similar results. Unable to refute him in a fair fight, "they" resort to slinging mud. Suborned witnesses allege that Stephen has spoken against Moses and God. These charges spark the first signs of popular opposition to the message. Another Sanhedrin trial results, before which Stephen is accused of claiming that Jesus will destroy the temple and modify the Torah.

Stephen answers these shocking charges (which will later be raised against Paul, 21:21) with the longest speech in Acts. Reasonable expectations that it will be among the most important summaries of Lukan theology seem at first unfulfilled. Rather than rebut the charges, Stephen appears to offer a long review of Sunday-school Bible history, which, if anything, lends credence to the charges. In fact, Stephen defends Christianity from the perspective of a family conflict within Judaism. In retrospect it is a masterpiece of malice, for its thesis is that large numbers of the chosen people have consistently blinded themselves to God's glory (7:2).

The speech stresses revelations and events that took place outside the borders of Palestine. When the members of the Sanhedrin callously ignore the glorious transfiguration displayed by Stephen throughout his speech (6:15; 7:56), they indicate their solidarity with their sinful forebears. Stephen's speech, like most of Luke-Acts, is largely biographical in structure, reviewing the lives of Abraham, Joseph, and Moses, culminating with the wilderness experience and the building of the temple. Readers will note close resemblances between the careers of these heroes and the life of Jesus. This last is thus the final reforming leader sent by God and rejected by his own.

The momentum of the speech gradually builds toward an attack. In the story of Joseph, family conflict comes to the fore, and the rejections of Moses strike home. The tone becomes shrill when recounting wilderness idolatry. The wilderness tent had a divine prototype. All thereafter was decline and fall, even the temple, which, whatever its merits, was no house needed by God. Stephen's view of sacred history is the typical perspective of reformers. His view of temples will be shared by Paul in Athens (7:48; 17:24), providing a learned basis for the unity of gentile and Jew. Stephen contends that any sins against Moses, Torah, and temple have been committed by the people as a whole. His closing invective demonstrates that the opportunity for repentance has expired.

This transfigured message leaves the audience transfixed with wrath. The speech that began with a revelation of God's glory closes with Stephen's personal vision of Jesus in glory (anticipating the fulfillment of Luke 22:69). The vision seals his fate. With ears stopped to protect its delicate sensibilities from such heresy, the Sanhedrin reconstitutes itself as a lynch mob, forgoing such technicalities as the delivery of a verdict and a sentence. Stephen dies with a nobility that confirms his message. Checking coats at the execution is a young man named Saul, who makes his initial (and only minor) appearance in Acts.

Stephen's death sounds the klaxon for a general persecution of the community. Only the apostles stand their ground; others flee. Pious Jews saw to the proper interment of Stephen's remains, as others of like heart had done for Jesus (Luke 23:50-56). Saul reacts quite differently, quickly emerging as the most zealous and rapacious of persecutors.

SUMMARY

In the space of these five fast-moving chapters, Luke has explained the origins of the Jewish-Christian rift, a continuation, in essence, of the opposition to Jesus. The originally supportive general public was manipulated into opposition. Its hatred lacks a rational base. Jealousy is its chief component, followed by the threat of loss of face for the Sanhedrin. The miracles wrought by Christian leaders are incontestable, and their arguments from Scripture stand against any attempt at refutation. Growth is the chief result of this malicious hatred. Ironically, the ultimate result of the persecution simply scattered the seeds from which new missions would bloom. The Diaspora looms on the horizon.

3

Breakout

8:4—15:35

Although the mission in Jerusalem will continue to prosper (21:20), Acts has finished its account of that work. The following chapters portray the gradual and divinely guided beginnings of the gentile mission. A series of conversion stories highlights this section. By interweaving various strands Luke demonstrates that Jerusalem ratified each step of this expansion. As the horizon moves outward, new characters come to the fore.

GREAT POWER IN SAMARIA (8:4-25)

While Paul continued his vicious oppression of the faithful, fugitives from the great persecution found new fields of endeavor. Philip seized the fallen mantle of Stephen and turned toward recalcitrant Samaria, moving a step beyond the Judaism centered upon the Jerusalem temple. Stephen's speech made such a move logical. Since Jesus himself had been rebuffed by the Samaritans (Luke 9:52-56), Philip's success is eloquent testimony to the effect of Pentecost.

Like Stephen and the apostles, Philip is a convincing preacher and worker of wonders. Demons flee and diseases disappear. A brief flashback recounts the career of one Simon, who had engaged in magical practice and had also awed the masses. In agreement with his own estimation of his ability, they hailed him as "the great power of God." (In the original Greek there is a wordplay, the "great miracles" of v. 13 being the plural of "great power." What Simon *claimed* to be, Philip could *do*.) Since the arrival of this competitor effectively ruined Simon's business, we expect some retaliation. Instead, we hear of the first of many individual conversions of note in this section. Simon submits to baptism. At this triumphal moment, Philip disappears from the story, to be replaced by others.

The Jerusalem apostles learn of this fresh enterprise and approve, dispatching Peter and John to the new field. Through their ministrations the gift of the Spirit is manifested. Simon (who as a magician was a connoisseur of such matters) suddenly exposes his unregenerate character by offering to purchase the secret of this technique from his patently superior fellow professionals. Magic is an important subject in Luke-Acts. The author does not claim that magic does not work, but that its origin is satanic. The defeat of magic and magicians actualizes the defeat of the devil. Magic also raises questions of the uses of power and money, symbolized in this instance by Simon's proposal and title. Magic involves the appropriation of supernatural force for personal ends. (If asked for a definition of "simony," Luke might reply that it is the charging of fees for sacramental and other ministries rather than the purchase of ecclesiastical office.)

Prompted by the fate of Ananias and Sapphira, the reader expects Simon's imminent demise. Instead he receives a summons to repentance, seasoned with grim warnings. Simon bids Peter to pray for him, and the story closes on an open note. Simon's future lay in his own hands, and his later history cannot be viewed as any fault of Peter's. Having finished their work in this Samaritan city, Peter and John return to Jerusalem, engaging in mission on the way. An old barrier has come down, together with a leader pursuing power and status.

A HAND TOWARD ETHIOPIA (8:26-39)

Philip now returns to center stage in a contrasting story. The eunuch from Ethiopia is the diametrical opposite of Simon, for he typifies the ideal potential believer, an ardent and open-minded reader of Scripture seeking a guide through its mysteries and the path to salvation. He is a true *theophilos* ("friend of God," 1:1).

Luke is also pleased to report that he is an exotic character, an African black of high status, an official in the court of his queen. Despite his prestige, the Ethiopian is condemned to hover on the margins of Judaism, debarred from full conversion by his physical condition.

Each step of this encounter is guided from above. As in the later story of Cornelius, an angel directs the scene. It opens with a surprising order to Philip to make his way toward the barren south, the desert, habitat of Israel in its pristine glory and the place of testing and revelation. While Philip carries out this directive, the scene shifts to the official and his enigma. Providentially, he has selected Isaiah 53 for his meditation. This raises perplexing questions, for which Philip can supply the answers. Their dialogue leads to an exposition of the gospel based upon Scripture. Water appears in the wilderness at an opportune moment. The eunuch has one more question. Torah forbade circumcision, but Baptism is available. When the sacrament has been administered, Philip is swept away in a rapture, but the Ethiopian journeys on, filled with Easter joy. Philip, too, travels on in missionary labors along the (largely gentile) coast, coming to a rest in Caesarea.

The story, with its fast action, exotic color, sentimental content, and mysterious but happy conclusion, has an immediate appeal. Beneath this pleasant surface structure lies a forest of symbols and allusions. These verses present the whole story of Acts in a nutshell and also encapsulate the experience of every believer. After Jerusalem, Judea, and Samaria (1:8), we have a foretaste of the ends of the earth, now revealed as a metaphor for the collapse of all boundaries. Its universal qualities gain strength from the atmosphere of romantic mystery provided by the personnel, the setting, and the supernatural movements and commands. Like the temptation of Jesus (Luke 4:1-11), the story occurs in a mythical world, cosmic and universal. Such a world invites the reader to identify and participate.

In structure the story of the Ethiopian closely resembles Luke 24:13-35. Each has a foundational meaning. What begins as a story about someone else's journey becomes the explication of *our* story and journey. The Ethiopian represents an important social group for

Luke: the "God-fearer," who is attracted to Judaism but unwilling to accept circumcision. Such "God-fearers" would have found themselves excluded from the temple. The Ethiopian is moving away from the place that would not accept him, but he does possess the Scripture and finds a catechist who belonged to the circle of one who insisted that "the Most High does not dwell in houses made with hands" (7:48).

The leading theme of the encounter is early Christian hermeneutics, exploration of the Scripture leading to answers for those who experience a barrier between themselves and the people of God. The gospel message encounters those engaged upon a spiritual journey with the offer of inclusion. The conversion of the Ethiopian is thus for Luke the "foundation myth" of gentile Christianity's origins among those condemned to the fringes of Judaism. It is symptomatic of Luke's genius that this foundational story is not only enjoyable in and of itself but also makes an important contribution to the plot. If, one may ask, this is parallel to the story of the journey to Emmaus, then why does it not occupy a similarly climactic place in the structure of Acts? In fact, it comes just as Luke reaches the heart of his tale.

OPENING THE EYES OF A BLIND MAN (9:1-31)

Luke now turns our attention from the Gaza trail to the Damascus road, from the conversion of a ready listener to the fate of a savage opponent. With a jar, joy suddenly gives way to rage, personified by the monstrous Saul, whose activities have chased the believers out of Jerusalem. Not satisfied with purging the holy city, Saul determines to pursue them into distant synagogues. This proposal receives official endorsement. In the course of this punitive journey from Jerusalem, Saul is struck with a bolt of heavenly light and the voice of Jesus, who has brought him to his knees and will bend him to Jesus' will. The blinded Saul must be led into the city he had intended to ravage without hindrance. For three days he languishes in the darkness of death, taking no food or drink.

Once more an enemy has felt the force of divine wrath. This is surely the most dramatic of all the punishment miracles in Acts and undoubtedly the most deserved. Death by starvation would be a fitting end to this very personification of rage. After he has passed three days in this spiritual tomb, however, providence intervenes. Our attention is fastened upon a Damascene believer named Ananias, who learns in a God-sent vision that Saul is at prayer and the recipient of a simultaneous vision depicting Ananias as his deliverer. Like the prophets of old, Ananias objects. Saul is just where he should be, implies Ananias, reminding the Deity of his numerous atrocities. An unconvinced God repeats the order, adding that Saul will be the chosen vessel to bear God's name to gentiles, monarchs, and Jews. In this dramatic setting we hear the clearest hint of a gentile mission yet, forecast by God. Its agent will be none other than the erstwhile scourge of Stephen and his circle.

So the persecutor becomes the persecuted. Saul leapt immediately into the fray, astonishing all. So successful is he in this new vocation that within a short time he becomes the target of a Jewish plot, from which he is cleverly extricated. Making his way to Jerusalem, Paul finishes the journey begun in 9:1. The perfect symmetry of 9:1-25 illustrates his 360-degree transformation: plot, blindness, conversion, initiation, commission, restored sight, and plot, beginning and closing in Jerusalem. The drama of the tale has contributed "Damascus road" to the repertory of English clichés. The stunning epiphany and the double dream leave no doubt that God is in charge of the play.

Saul's adventures in Jerusalem repeat and reinforce those in Damascus. The apostles are no less skeptical than was Ananias. Barnabas becomes an intermediary, thus initiating an important friendship. The convert takes up where Stephen had left off, and would certainly have suffered his fate had the plot not been detected and its intended victim been sent off to safety in Tarsus. The defection of this great persecutor brought tranquility and growth to the faithful in Judea, Galilee (mentioned only in this note), and Samaria. These are, with Jerusalem, three of the four places listed in 1:8. Only the ends of the earth remain.

TWO WHO DIDN'T STAY IN BED (9:32-43)

Peter returns to the fore. Following, as in Samaria, the path of Philip, he arrives in Lydda, there encountering a cripple. Unlike the detailed healing reported earlier, the story rushes ahead with few details. To this paralytic named Aeneas, Peter addresses the message that liberates and empowers: "Rise and make your bed." The ability to make up his cot would symbolize his transition from dependence to self-sufficiency. (Fortunately, however, Luke spares us from generations of moralizing approaches by neglecting to report that the bed was actually made.) The impact of the story is inversely proportional to the economy and brevity of its narration, for it leads to the conversion of an entire region.

Leaving Peter there, the narrative moves to the coast to tell of a wealthy and pious leader of the community at Joppa, Tabitha, who was apparently a widow. No sooner does her story begin than it appears to end, with an abrupt report of illness and death. As burial preparations are under way, it is discovered that Peter is near by, and emissaries summon him in haste, presumably to conduct the obsequies for this local pillar. When the apostle arrives he is conducted into the presence of the departed and confronted by an upper room filled with lamenting widows exhibiting the products of their industry, which had been aided and subsidized by Tabitha. Her loss has been an economic disaster for them. While we are still feeling the pathos and are smiling at the picture of Peter attempting to make appropriate comments regarding these garments about which he, an ignorant male, knows nothing, the apostle orders the room cleared, not because he is vexed at the widows, but for secrecy. After praying on bended knee, he addresses the corpse with the same word directed at Aeneas: "Rise." She does and is presently restored to the company of her fellow widows and believers. As might be expected, this miracle produces numerous conversions, and Peter takes up residence in Joppa with a local tanner.

These two little stories provide a transition between, and a foil to, the momentous accounts preceding and following. But they are more than filler. They are reminiscent of Luke 8:40-56 and thus attest to the ongoing ministry of Jesus in the church. Healing and rebirth also serve to summarize the experiences of the Ethiopian and of Saul, and to set the tone for what is coming. Men and women, wealthy widows and cripples, even those with pagan names, have felt the gospel's force. The story of Tabitha symbolizes the heavenly treasures laid up by those who are fervent in works of charity. Furthermore, these deeds have left Peter strategically placed for his next endeavor.

THE CONVERSION OF PETER—AND OTHERS (10:1—11:18)

Leaving Peter in Joppa, we journey to Caesarea and the home of another pious almsgiver, Cornelius, a centurion who has nearly everything in common with Tabitha except his sex, which is irrelevant, and his race, which is relevant. On the fringes of Palestine he hovers on the fringes of Judaism. Jesus also had dealings with a centurion (Luke 7:2-10) of similar quality. There the boundary between Jew and Gentile stood firm. Centurions were not ancient noncoms (sergeants). Upon retirement they could move into town aristocracies. Persons of this quality could give tone to a movement and could provide substantial resources and support.

The importance of this story becomes apparent in its resemblance to the opening of Luke's Gospel, which also presented an angelic visitation in the midst of cultic piety. The message delivered to Cornelius hints that his prayers are no less efficacious than is sacrifice. Following this affirmation, the angel directs that Cornelius send for Peter, whose name and address are supplied (cf. 9:10-11). Baffled Cornelius complies, wondering what this is all about. We happily suspect what will happen and can enjoy his suspense.

By 3 P.M. the next day, the delegation sent by Cornelius was approaching Joppa, and the camera shifts in mid-sentence to Peter, who is, of course, at prayer (cf. 3:1), on a rooftop in accordance with pious custom. He was hungry. Luke certainly does not wish to imply autosuggestion, so such minutiae require some reflection. Not now, however, for Peter is swept into a trance and sees an object descending from the open heaven. Recalling the Baptism of Jesus (Luke 3:21-22) the language proclaims a great revelation. The vision is elaborate and fascinating. Within the confines of something like a linen receptacle, appear the various animal species, described in the words of Gen. 1:24-25 and evoking the goodness of all creation. Before Peter can begin to interpret, a voice (cf. again the Baptism) commands him to slaughter and eat these creatures. Peter rejects this order to violate Torah. The voice demands that he dare not call impure what God has made clean. Does this abolish the distinction of foods? How have they been made pure? We, too, are puzzled. Three times the command is given, and three times refused, after which the object ascends. Has Peter, like Jesus, thrice rebuffed satanic temptation, or has he once more thrice denied his Lord? Gentile readers may sense the dilemma, but they pray for Peter to change his mind.

As in the case of Saul and Ananias, two persons have received visions, but here the connection is elusive. While Peter struggled with this puzzle, the emissaries of Cornelius opportunely arrived. The Spirit now instructs Peter to go with them "without hesitation." The phrase is ambiguous, meaning also "no distinctions" or "no discrimination." Given his recent obstinacy, the advice is not impractical. Peter will not listen to another gospel, even from an angel in heaven. He does listen to the Spirit and thus learns the cause of the visit. The hospitality he offers is an encouraging sign. The wagon is beginning to roll, but only upon the single wheel of Cornelius's vision. Peter's own experience lingers in limbo.

A large delegation departs Joppa the next day, swollen by the addition of believers from that city, who will serve as witnesses. The journey takes two days. As time for their arrival draws near, the expectant Cornelius assembled family and close friends. When Peter began to cross the threshold separating gentile from Jew, the Roman officer cast himself at his feet. This reversal of social roles was theologically inappropriate, of course, and refused, but the gesture shows that Cornelius recognized an epiphany. The two immediately engage in friendly conversation as they enter the house to face the crowd. At no loss for words, Peter explains his action by reference to the vision (10:28). This is the decisive breakthrough, interpretation reached through reflection upon revelation in the context of experience. By seeing the vision as an allegory, Peter has crossed another threshold and is in the process of his own conversion, scarcely less important than that of Saul (cf. Luke 24:45).

The floor is now given to Cornelius, who repeats, and thus emphasizes, his vision, the results of which have now come to pass. Accepting the invitation to speak, Peter makes his missionary address to gentiles (as will Paul, 17:16-34). The speech is brief and symmetrical, framed by a statement that God summons all people. Within this context Jesus is described as "Lord of all" (v. 36). His cosmic role over creation has missionary and dietary implications. This short sermon (vv. 36-43) contains the only "biography" of Jesus in Acts, in a style like that used by Stephen to portray Joseph and Moses. Jesus was a benefactor anointed by God to aid the victims of satanic tyranny.

As Peter begins to expound the message of the death and resurrection, his speech is interrupted, not by the police (4:1), but by the Holy Spirit, who showers the benefits of Pentecost upon Cornelius and his household. This is indeed a new beginning. The Jewish onlookers express amazement, while Peter draws the inevitable conclusion. After having the group baptized, Peter accepts Cornelius's kind invitation to linger. This will strengthen the bonds of their fellowship and allow time for word of this turn of affairs to percolate up to Jerusalem. When, in his own good time, Peter returned, he was taken to task by "those of the circumcision," an anachronism so jarring that it reveals the circumstances of later conflicts.

The burden of their complaint was not that he had ordered the baptism of Gentiles, but that he had associated and eaten with them. To these charges, apparently set out in the course of a community assembly, Peter replies with a speech recapitulating the events of chap. 10. Since Luke is quite capable of summarizing, we must regard the detailed description as a means for providing emphasis.

Fortunately Peter had brought along with him the six believing Jews from Joppa to corroborate his story, which was accepted deferentially and without objection. The conclusion in 11:18 echoes the opening in 11:1. The admission of gentiles is a cause for gratitude and praise to the God who works wonders. On this triumphant note the ministry of Peter in Acts draws to an end. He has one more adventure to undergo, but he will not be brought back to play an official role until chap. 15, where he will in his final words recollect this episode. Its sixty-six verses make this story the longest within Acts. The use of emphatic repetition, the presence of visions and visitations, and the scenic structure with detailed chronology are devices employed to stress its importance. The first conversion of a gentile took place under the auspices of Peter, the leading apostle, who, far from rushing precipitously into this venture, had to be prodded by the Spirit. The initial gentile convert, moreover, was not some nameless face from the crowd but a person of high standing and considerable influence, an individual noteworthy for piety and rectitude.

Since Peter has shown no lack of initiative and Cornelius could scarcely have been a shrinking violet, their passive roles in this account lend testimony to Luke's need to stress the hand of God behind all this. The origin of the gentile mission remained controversial into Luke's own day. Peter has opened the gates. Now the flood will pour forth.

SOME NOTABLE CONTRASTS (11:19—12:25)

At this juncture Luke reaches down to pick up threads left dangling since 8:4, returning to the account of others scattered by the great persecution. Their mission extended to the coast (cf. Philip and Peter), then north (to Tyre and Sidon?), east to Cyprus, and finally to the Syrian metropolis of Antioch. Jews alone had been evangelized until certain Cypriots and Cyrenians (we read of Barnabas and Mnason from Cyprus, 4:36 and 21:16, and of Lucius from Cyrene, 13:1) began to convert gentiles, with great success and signs of divine favor. Jerusalem heard of this progress and sent Barnabas to demonstrate its leadership and approval, precisely as had been done through Peter and John in the case of Samaria.

This merits what amounts to a new introduction for Barnabas. He is so successful that he requires assistance and takes thought of Saul, whom he visits in Tarsus to recruit. They labor a full year in Antioch—a long time in Acts. In fact, the term "Christian" (which Luke does not favor) originated in Antioch.

Onto this happy scene there eventually arrive "prophets from Jerusalem." As usual (except for the Seven), Luke does not describe the origin and installation of new officers, but shows them in action. Agabus provides the example, foretelling a catastrophe of apocalyptic proportions—a universal famine. The author intervenes to state that this famine did happen, during the reign of Claudius.

Believers do not regard this as a sign of the coming end, but take up a collection for transmission to Jerusalem, selecting Barnabas and Saul as their agents. They will deliver it to elders, not apostles. Thus does the new gentile church link itself to the founding community through an act of service, *diakonia* (an expression used earlier for "ministry"). Their loyalty to Jerusalem is commendable, for a universal famine will affect them no less than their fellows in Judea. Through this event we also learn of a changed situation in which elders rule the church and prophets have become officers. Barnabas and Saul discharge their mission and return at 12:25, but not before some interesting events have occurred.

Acts 12:1 brings a drastic change of tone, beginning with the summary of a tragic and shocking death. Herod killed James (the brother of John) with the sword. Since the death of Stephen has been reported in detail, there is no need for verbiage here. Moreover, this brief narration leaves no room for heroic exposition. James followed his master to death. Nothing more need be said. The act itself raises suspense. This Herod does not play games. (The readers of Acts would presumably regard this king as the wicked tyrant of the gospel tradition.) The famine and killing together fulfill the prediction of Jesus at Luke 21:11-13.

Herod was not insensitive to public opinion (a quality that would lead to his downfall). Seeing the good reviews produced by his execution of James, he determined to add Peter as an encore. Out of deference to the holidays, however, he kept him in prison for a time, under the most stringent conditions attainable, to prevent a recurrence of the unpleasantness that had marred an earlier meeting of the Sanhedrin (5:17-25). Passover provides more than suspense, of course. With the phrase "the days of unleavened bread" Luke recalls the passion of Christ and invokes a literal interpretation of the need for disciples to imitate their teachers. Then there is the acrid irony of selecting the feast of liberation from bondage as a time for chains and death. While others keep the feast, Peter lies in chains, guarded by four shifts of four soldiers, two of whom attend him always. These conditions left little room for hope, but the community continues its ardent prayer (cf. 4:23-31).

Rightly so, for at the very last moment God intervenes. An angel of the Lord bursts upon the scene amid a blaze of light (cf. Luke 2:9, Acts 9:3). This is an epiphany. Yet Peter continues to sleep soundly, at peace despite his impending death. The angel rouses him with a kick in the side, adding words that recall the raising of the dead (as in 9:40-41). At this moment the chains fall away. A maddening dialogue ensues, with the angel overseeing each stage of Peter's dressing. Why cannot he finish these preparations after escaping? When the angel is finally satisfied with his wardrobe, their exit begins. As in the case of the conversion of Cornelius, heavenly directives govern every single step.

Peter, we learn, did not know what was happening, but imagined that this was all a dream. Dreaming or whatever, the pair must negotiate their way through a series of guards posted to prevent any escape. The most awesome barrier of all comes at the end: an iron door. This opens magically before them. The angel escorts Peter for a block, then vanishes. The apostle is on his own, but not home free. Realizing that he really has escaped, he sets out for the house of Mary, apparently a wealthy widow, better known to a later generation as John Mark's mother. In this Greek-speaking house church a group had gathered for prayer. It presents one more locked door to pass. Peter must risk rousing attention by pounding upon it. A slave named Rose came to his knock. All but hysterical with excitement at the sight of one risen from the dead (cf. Luke 24:41), she unwisely leaves the all too recognizable apostle out in the cold to rush back with the good news.

Peter is redeeming the debt incurred in a previous courtyard encounter with a maid (Luke 22:56). Rose in turn is greeted like the women who had brought Peter and others news of the empty tomb (Luke 24:11). When she persists, the community gathered to pray for his release reveals their conviction that this prayer will not be granted. They propose that flighty Rose has seen his guardian angel, as may happen after death. Her report thus confirms the execution. While this theological debate proceeds, Peter must linger in the street amid increasing danger that someone will pop out to see what these suspicious Christians are up to now. As he pounds away on the door, they contrive a solution: see who is at the door. Once recognized, Peter hastily silences them and delivers a brief account of the rescue with a commission to announce it to James and the believers. He then withdraws to an undisclosed location.

The escape caused quite a flurry at the prison, and Herod did not receive the news gladly. After investigation he had the guards executed and then, like Peter, went to another place. In this case it was Caesarea, scene of recent events. Another quarrel arises, this time with the citizens of Tyre and Sidon. Being civilized, they sue for peace. Moreover, they depend upon grain from Herod's lands to survive. Their overtures follow the customary procedure observed in Hellenistic principalities and take the form of "persuading" his chamberlain, Blastus. Those who sense corruption are not on the wrong track. The ensuing reconciliation called for a celebration. Herod donned his regal vestments (cf. Peter's earlier dressing) and presented an oration so successful that it is hailed as an epiphany (cf. v. 7), as is he. Whereas Peter had imagined that he was dreaming, the crowd is deluded into imagining that it sees divinity. Herod now has his turn for a kick from an angel, this an instrument of punishment for the usurpation of divine glory. In the manner of tyrants he dies writhing with an infestation of worms.

While Herod was receiving this due reward, foiled in his attempts to persecute and being doomed to a wretched death, Christians flourished. Barnabas and Saul returned, having finished their mission of mercy.

This chapter is a Lukan masterpiece, pleasing on the surface and dense with cross-references and layers of meaning. The initial and concluding references to the offering from Antioch frame the account with Christian benefaction, strongly contrasted to the supposed "benefactions" of tyrannical despots, who, having concocted a dispute, resolve it by accepting bribes and then rejoice to be hailed as saviors and benefactors. Herod "rescued" Tyre and Sidon from an artificially contrived famine; humble believers share meager resources to relieve a genuine famine. The two stories provide an exegesis by example of Luke 22:25. No less edifying are the contrasting fates of Peter and Herod, the latter meeting the fate he had designed for the former. Their stories unfold in inverse symmetry, punctuated by ironic parallels.

In Peter's final appearance of substance, he experiences a sort of passion and resurrection, complete with arrest, imprisonment, delivery, appearance to incredulous followers, farewell commission, and mysterious departure. "Bonds" and "prison" are common symbols for death, as is "light" for rebirth. There are numerous parallels with Luke 22—24. Paschal images are also apparent. Herod plays the part of the wicked pharaoh, from whose "hand" (cf. Exod. 14:30) Peter is rescued by the angel of the Lord. Peter's dressing gains significance from Exod. 12:11 and 15:4. Luke had characterized the passion-resurrection of Jesus as *exodos* (especially in the transfiguration story, which also has points of contact with Acts 12, including sleep and light).

The passion/passover references give this story a universal quality. A paradigmatic understanding gains profile from recognition of many initiatory motifs: sleep (= death), enlightenment, rising, putting on garments, crossing boundaries (the *limina* between wilderness and promised land, life and death, old and new), and the helplessness of Peter, who acts like a newborn babe. Through these symbols the story recapitulates the rebirth and redemption of every Christian in baptism. Those so reborn also hear the fateful call of v. 8: "Follow me." Both James and Peter obeyed that command to discipleship. Further attention to parallels brings to mind the story of Jonah, by which this account is linked to Paul's experiences in chap. 27, and such prophetic texts as Ezek. 28:1-10 and Isa. 14:12-20.

Despite the thickness of allusion and parallel, this passage is filled with suspense, humor, and excitement, crammed with a multitude of characters from monarch to slave, and enlivened with easily perceptible ironies and contrasts, crowned in the end with two happy results. Acts 12 is a series of Chinese boxes, with something for everyone and more than a little for most. While prisoners shed their bonds (Luke 4:18), and the mighty are put down from their thrones (Luke 1:52), the bonds between Jewish and gentile believers grow stronger, and Jerusalem is established as the chair. Finally, Luke has quietly suggested a transition in leadership. Prophets and elders appear, together with James, the new leader, and John Mark of

Jerusalem. Peter, having opened the door of faith to gentiles and passed through prison gates, may retire.

MAKING STRAIGHT THE PATH (13:1-13)

Acts 13 begins with a list, a signal of an important transition (1:13, 6:5, 20:3). Acts 13:1-3 forms an inclusion with 14:23-28, setting off the unit we call "the first missionary journey" (although Luke does not use the expression). This section begins and ends at Antioch, as previous sections had opened and closed at Jerusalem, an indication that the story has a new axis. Jerusalem remains the holy and mother city, but it is no longer the center of the story.

The leadership at Antioch contains prophets and teachers, the latter office new to readers, and includes a black, a resident of present-day Libya, a Cypriot of Levitic origins, a onetime accomplice of Herod the Tetrarch, and a resident of Tarsus. While they are engaged in prayer during the course of a fast, the voice of the Spirit is heard. The Spirit continues to point to new directions, but for the first time the impetus for mission comes through the agency of a community. Following an impressive ceremony, Barnabas and Saul go forth, taking Mark as an assistant.

They visit Cyprus and move across the island from west to east. Luke reports no results but stresses concentration upon synagogues. The priorities of salvation history have not changed. Luke illustrates the entire mission with a single story. Just as Jesus had begun his Spirit-filled ministry in an encounter with the devil (Luke 4:1-11) and Peter found his first mission journey climaxed by his denunciation of Simon, so, on his first journey, Saul must face a satanic agent, one Bar-Jesus (whose name really means "false prophet," not "son of Joshua," Luke tells us). This creature had found a very good living as a sort of domestic chaplain to the Roman governor, Sergius Paulus, a discerning man who presented an invitation to Barnabas and Saul. Roman governors did not conduct receptions on street corners, and we can imagine a palatial setting. Their presentation must have been effective, for deceiving Bar-Jesus, seeing his employment threatened, attempted to make a refutation. However skilled he may have been at theological debate we shall never know, for *Paul*, as he is now identified, lays upon him an elaborate curse, revealing in a flash his own oratorical ability and spiritual power. The (Jewish) magician is reduced to the state of the vanquished persecutor (9:8). Blinding is a normal form of divine punishment, but it was also one of the chief weapons in a magician's arsenal. In addition to this suitable irony, Paul refers to "making crooked the straight paths of the Lord" (v. 10), thus recalling the beginnings of another ministry that would lead to universal salvation (Luke 3:5-6). The proconsul took counsel of his spiritual life and converted.

The opening of this new endeavor is thus marked by the symbolic defeat of Satan and an exemplary conversion. Luke's readers would have thrilled at reading that Sergius Paulus had adopted their faith. Proconsuls did not routinely affiliate with lowbrow or revolutionary sects. At the climax of Paul's missionary career there will come another triumph over Jewish deceivers, magical practice, and the like, together with friendship displayed by the highly placed (chap. 19). Luke has artfully arranged the structure of Acts. He shows the advance of the kingdom by telling paradigmatic stories that symbolize its impact. If this seems untoward, one could appeal to Jesus, who also proclaimed the coming and meaning of the kingdom by telling stories.

Luke does not usually work by making such statements as "during the course of the mission on Cyprus, Paul emerged as the real leader." Instead, he prefers to *show* rather than tell. Paul suddenly vaults into leadership, revealing at the same time his Roman name while ridding a gubernatorial palace of barbarous superstition. By 13:13 Barnabas has been obliterated ("Paul and his company"), and Mark has had enough. Under this new inspiration the mission leaps forward, traversing immense and formidable distances (at least to those who can look at relief maps) to land after a single bound in the synagogue of Antioch at Pisidia, a Roman colony in the heart of present-day Turkey.

SOWING THE SEED (13:14-52)

Paul, like Jesus, follows a defeat of Satan with a debut in the synagogue. This sermon and its aftermath have many correspondences to Luke 4:16-30. Here also the service is described, climaxing with an invitation to the strangers to preach. Paul accepts in their behalf. Unlike Jesus, who sat, Paul assumes the standing position of the orator. This is the Diaspora. Fortunately for the course of the story, Paul will be able to continue this practice of synagogue preaching, despite growing opposition.

This sermon also bears some resemblances to Peter's Pentecost address. Although not an apostle, Paul preaches an authentic gospel. The sermon reviews the promises of salvation history, proclaims their fulfillment, and summons the hearers to respond. The first section conveniently picks up the thread of sacred history where Stephen had left off, avoiding repetition and providing the reader with a continuous sequence. Also like Stephen, Paul unfolds a gradually mounting criticism of the Jewish people, although it is more subdued. The closing verses (39-41) foreshadow opposition.

Within the audience is a new element, "those who fear God," non-Jews like Cornelius and the Ethiopian, who are attracted to the faith. Paul makes overtures to these God-fearers. The sermon was a huge success, leading the exiting worshipers to plead for more next week. A horde of Jews and converts attached themselves to the missionaries. For seven days anticipation and suspense mount. When the Sabbath finally arrived, nearly the entire populace had gathered to hear more. The sight of this throng, larger than any synagogue could contain, inflamed the Jews with jealousy, leading them to repudiate the teachings of Paul and, in their zeal, to transgress the bounds of religious propriety. Quite unintimidated, Paul and Barnabas, like Peter and John before the Sanhedrin, boldly deliver judgment. To the chosen people the promise was made, and it was fulfilled. Because they have no regard for eternal life, the gentiles will have their turn. The citation of Isa. 49:6 shows that this is no innovation. In this dramatic context Luke 2:32 is recalled, as readers perceive that "the ends of the earth" are both geographical and symbolic, for the ends in view are God's goals for the salvation of all. The emergence of this light to the nations does not shock us, because Luke has, since chap. 1, been slowly raising the wick, allowing our eyes gradually to acclimatize themselves to the situation.

Confronted by the resultant brushfire of gentile conversions, the outraged Jews approach their women sympathizers, who, we may presume, work their wiles upon their highly placed husbands. Pillow talk leads to persecution and expulsion of the troublesome pair (cf. Luke 4:28-30). In accordance with Jesus' instructions (Luke 10:10-12), the two remove all traces of the offending city from their feet. As they set out for Iconium we take a last reassuring glimpse at the faithful who, amid persecution, manifest Easter joy.

The same pattern of success, Jewish resistance, announcement of judgment, and its result, recurs twice more in vv. 44-52. The events at Antioch have a paradigmatic character and will be repeated again and again. Paul begins in the synagogue. His success sparks Jewish resistance, which takes the form of futile attempts to squash the mission, thus justifying the shift to gentiles. This turn provokes more intense opposition and still greater success. Rather than strangle the movement, persecution serves as the catapult from which it is propelled from one location to another. When 13:47 is recalled at 28:25-28, it becomes apparent that the essence of the plot was contained in chap. 13. Frequent repetition certainly drives home the point for Christian readers and presents "the Jews" as driving one nail after another into the coffin of their religious heritage.

BARBARIANS CAN BE FICKLE (14:1-23)

Acts 14:1-7 bears this out. After their arrival at Iconium, Paul and Barnabas make the synagogue their base, persuading a large number of Jews as well as gentiles. In the face of opposition from hostile Jews, they bravely persist in a ministry attested by signs and wonders, like that of Jesus and the apostles. The Iconians soon manifest the factionalism that plagued Greek cities. In the course of time the whole populace had taken one side or the other. Both Jewish and gentile leaders oppose the movement, leaving the missionaries on thin ice. Fortunately a plot to take them in a rush and pelt them with stones is detected, enabling the two to elude their enemies and escape to the region of Lystra and Derbe. Suspense grows with the mention of this vicious plan. How long will they be able to avoid the long arms of stone-throwing Iconians?

After all this tersely narrated excitement, the story finally lets up. At Lystra Paul meets, then heals, a cripple in an account reassuringly similar to the stories of earlier deeds wrought by Jesus and Peter (Luke 5:18-26, Acts 3:1-9). The crowd responds with the usual excitement, but it is soon clear that the miracle has been rather too successful. These volatile rustics, who do not even speak Greek when stirred up, conclude that the pair before them are gods and prepare suitable veneration. Because Luke thoughtfully translates the Lycaonian speech for us, we know what is going on. Paul and Barnabas, however, do not, and the proceedings are allowed to reach a blasphemous juncture. We do not, of course, approve of the regrettable pagan inclination to blur the border between human and divine, but we may enjoy seeing how Paul struck those whom he encountered.

The story also involves a bit of fun at the expense of the locals. Learned readers of Luke's time were likely to have been familiar with an ancient legend describing the visit of Zeus and Hermes, in mufti, to Phrygia. The natives were not hospitable to these apparent strangers, who met cold receptions in mortal guise until, at long last, they came upon a decrepit and elderly couple, Baucis and Philemon, who happily offered to share their pathetically meager resources. The Phrygians had taken a lot of ribbing for this gaucherie, and they were determined to demonstrate their amendment of life. This explains their somewhat hasty rush to deify the two strangers, whose deed indicated that Zeus and Hermes were up to their old tricks.

Once they discover what is about to happen, Paul and Barnabas do not smile, but rush in to avert this sacrilege with a joint proclamation of the God whose miracles abound every day. This speech offers a kind of preview of the Areopagus address (17:22-31). Every bit of elegance and acumen was needed to stave off disaster. In this amusing incident Luke gives a vivid picture of the enormous challenges faced by missionaries attempting to transform pagans into Christians. The theology presented in 14:15-17 would most likely appeal to those with some education and intellectual aspirations, enhancing the rather haughty tone of the whole episode toward vulgar superstitions. We also note that pagan ignorance is much more venial than that of the Jerusalem Jews.

Further evidence of the volatility of these barbarians emerges in v. 19, as the emotional pendulum swings from attempted deification to attempted assassination. The impetus for this shift came from a pack of Iconian Jews, who, having picked up reinforcements from Antioch, had endured a lengthy journey over rugged terrain to bring Paul to ground. Hastening upon the scene, they quickly transformed the adoring crowd into a lynch mob. Battering Paul with volleys of rocks, they dragged his corpse out of the city limits (corpses defile), and dumped it there. Then, presumably, tired but pleased with a good day's work, they returned to their peace-loving homes. In any event, they left the field to a timid band of believers who there gathered to surround the lacerated body of the fallen evangelist whose funeral they must now plan. In the midst of their tribulation rises an astonishing sight: Paul! Battered and bleeding as he was, he had not been cowed, for rather than seek shelter in safety elsewhere, he returned to the city. The very next day, unhindered by bruises and wounds, he set out for Derbe. That is some kind of heroism. Barnabas also left with him, now so overshadowed by Paul that the mob had left him unmolested.

After a profitable mission at Derbe, unpunctuated by any report of resistance, Paul and Barnabas courageously revisit each site in which they had labored (with the exception of Cyprus; cf. 15:39). Paul's pastoral work comes briefly into focus, as he cares for established congregations and ordains local leaders. Having circled back through their path, Paul and Barnabas return to Antioch and report upon their achievements. The response recalls 11:18. Paul and Barnabas stay in Antioch for some time, and word of their success reaches Jerusalem, where, it will appear, not all share their joy.

MANAGING CONFLICT (15:1-35)

A dissonant note breaks into the joyous song of celebration intoned at Antioch when some anonymous Judeans, whose authorization remains vague, arrive and promulgate the doctrine that circumcision is necessary for salvation. This leads to a certain want of harmony and engages Paul and Barnabas in heated debate with them. The community determines to send an embassy to Jerusalem to meet with the apostles and elders. Internal dissent once again threatens the community. This dispute upsets and surprises the reader, who has been given to understand that the whole matter had been settled following the conversion of Cornelius. In the course of their subsequent journey the delegation, headed naturally by Paul and Barnabas, made stops in Phoenicia and Samaria, where word of success among gentiles elicited great joy. Jerusalem also gave them a formal welcome, although the note of joy is noticeably absent. Suspense rises. Some believing Pharisees advanced their view that circumcision and Torah observance are necessary. Are these Pharisees new adherents of the faith? We do not know. Their demand is formally separated from what is in 15:6, the description of an official meeting.

That demand, moreover, lacks one important feature of the doctrine proclaimed at Antioch: Torah observance is not presented as necessary for salvation. It has no soteriological effect. A small gap has opened. Through it the bandwagon of church unity may safely pass.

A lively debate ensued. By leaving its contents and participants to the reader's imagination, Luke permits us to share in the story. This also removes any possible distraction from the roles the leaders will play. First into the fray stepped Peter, who reminded the audience of the precedent set long ago in the conversion of Cornelius. God sanctioned that action. Jews and gentiles are both saved by God's beneficent grace. Peter closed with an implicit warning, not unlike the threats often issued to Jewish audiences: "Beware lest you put God to the test."

Having quelled the controversy with these Gamaliel-like words, Peter may now pass the torch to James. Before that torch is taken up the community has opportunity to listen respectfully to Paul and Barnabas list the miracles that attested their labors. Those who wish to hear Paul refute "Judaizers" will have to turn elsewhere. This is James's hour.

The new head takes the floor to give his stamp of approval to the words of his colleague, Peter. James then goes on to state for the

first time in Acts the explicit theological principle justifying a gentile
mission: gentiles may be enrolled among the people of God. Scripture is congruent with the experience of the Spirit, as a lengthy
citation from Amos confirms. James joins Peter in presenting the
gentile mission as the result of a hermeneutical breakthrough—the
mind-opening impact of Easter. The fulfillment of the promises of
a Davidic reign has taken shape, not in the form of a world empire,
but in the possibility of messianic salvation becoming available to
all.

James is in charge and demonstrates this by delivering the conclusion to be reached. Gentile believers will not be harassed. They
will, however, have to observe four customs widely promulgated
by the public reading of the Torah, customs binding upon gentile
sojourners in the promised land. Eucharistic fellowship is possible
under these conditions. By not answering directly at that time the
question raised about eating with gentiles at 11:3, and by avoiding
in the pronouncement of James any reference to forbidden species,
Luke has preserved the coherence of his account and the integrity
of Peter's vision.

Without a hint of any need for debate, the whole body resolved
to communicate this decree in the form of an official letter to be
transmitted to Antioch by the hands of a formal delegation. Judas
Barsabbas and Silas will serve as envoys. On this dignified note the
most elaborate account of a church meeting in Acts comes to a
solemn end. Luke's early readers would have been impressed at the
official quality of these proceedings and their resemblance to a civic
assembly, complete with officers, plenary sessions, crisp resolutions,
and official letters. Most impressive of all was the genteel atmosphere of the debate, guided by wise leaders heard in silence and
with consideration. Once again, a problem has been solved through
prompt action directed by efficient and able leaders supported by a
responsive and decorous membership. This meeting shows how little
the Christians have in common with the vast throngs of unwashed
rabble who packed theaters to howl their grievances. Standing in
the middle of the book, this meeting is its centerpiece in every sense
of that word.

Acts 15:30-35, in reversing the itinerary of vv. 1-5, also reverses the situation. Conflict has given way to consolation, turmoil to peace. On this happy note the delegates make their farewells to Antioch. By 15:35 Paul and Barnabas find themselves once again in the pleasant circumstances that marked the end of chap. 14. Managed conflicts lead to growth.

SUMMARY

The apparently haphazard missionary efforts sparked by the great persecution have prospered. Philip labored in Samaria and found his plans endorsed by Jerusalem. His conversion of the Ethiopian offers glittering prospects, realized in the mission of Peter to Cornelius. The defeat of the leading persecutor removed an obstacle and added a potent resource, whose abilities emerged at Damascus, Jerusalem, and (later) in the new gentile mission center at Antioch. Jerusalem blessed this effort also, sending Barnabas to assist. Neither famine nor persecution slowed the momentum. Soon the wind of the Spirit wafted Paul and Barnabas onto a far-flung journey, marked by rising Jewish opposition and subsequent success among gentiles. The presence of the latter precipitated a quarrel, quickly settled at Jerusalem. The way is now clear for an unhindered mission to Jews and gentiles alike. At the conclusion of the previous chapter, Paul, then Saul, was ravaging the church. In the present chapter his rise to prominence in the Christian movement has taken place. Hereafter he will be on his own. Peter is out of the picture, and the Jerusalem church, now led by James, emerges only when Paul visits. He is the light to the gentiles. On him Luke's beacon will rest.

4

Paul: Light to the Nations

15:36—19:40

This section begins in the aftermath of the model Christian assembly portrayed in chap. 15 and closes with the tumultuous Ephesian "assembly" of chap. 19. Paul ventures into new territories where, despite persistent and not fruitless efforts to convert Jews, he will experience his greatest success among gentiles. The principal speech of this unit is thus the famous Areopagus address to gentile pagans (17:22-31), whereas in the previous chapter his showcase sermon was addressed to Jews in the Pisidian synagogue (13:16-41). The Jerusalem decision has opened a door through which Paul will shortly pass.

A SLOW START (15:36—16:10)

The beginnings of this adventure are hardly auspicious. Like the journey of Peter that eventuated in the conversion of Cornelius, it takes root in a modest proposal to engage in a pastoral visit. When Barnabas suggests that the pair once again make use of the services of John Mark, Paul demurs. The resultant dispute had a happy issue, for the work became two-pronged, Barnabas and Mark heading for Cyprus, and Paul through Syria and Cilicia with a new colleague of his own choosing, Silas. The latter, like Barnabas, had come from Jerusalem. Paul's selection of him reflects his new authority. They embark with the community's blessings. Changes of personnel often foreshadow changes of direction. As Barnabas sails off the pages of Acts we may regret the departure of this important and honorable personality, but Luke's history sails with Paul. The contrast with 13:1-3 is also marked by the absence of direction from the Spirit. Antioch is no longer in charge of Paul.

In the course of his delivery of the decree, Paul presently arrives at Lystra. Apparently desirous of another assistant, he learns that a certain Timothy comes with distinguished local recommendations. Paul thus circumcises this product of a mixed marriage. In the light of chap. 15 this seems surprising, but reflection suggests that it was done with an eye to missionary strategy. By this act Paul witnesses to his commitment to the priority of the Jewish mission. It also neatly anticipates a criticism later leveled (21:21). The three then continue on their task of instituting the decree of Jerusalem. In fact, Luke tends to prefer the singular. Paul is the central character, his assistants playing menial and shadowy roles.

When they reach fresh fields in central Asia Minor, the Spirit takes a hand, forbidding new missionary work. This inhibition remains in force until they have reached the coast. Modern readers may not easily appreciate the vast amount of territory traversed since 15:36, a journey fraught with the rigors of ancient overland travel. We do not appreciate it because Luke relegates this arduous journey to a summary, building suspense as we wait for something important to happen.

At Acts 16:10 it does. From this point on, revelations come only to Paul or about Paul. The first of these is also the most dramatic, a nocturnal vision of a Macedonian summoning him to "help us." Such visions were vouchsafed to leaders like Alexander the Great or Caesar to presage a momentous turn of events. So it must be in this instance. The vision portends events no less significant than the conversion of Cornelius. Far from the environs of Antioch and Jerusalem, Paul stands poised on the fringes of Europe.

At this critical juncture Luke introduces the most mysterious of those puzzles by which he entices and challenges the reader: the occasional use of "we," with its implications of personal presence. Efforts to tag the scope of this usage and file it safely away are probably futile. Formally, it is common in travel accounts, especially in sea travel, but Luke does not thus absolutely restrict its use.

Geographically, it is prominent in the Aegean coastal region, but not limited thereto. Thematically, it emphasizes major moments and events. Literarily, the "we" brings readers into the story. Its intimacy makes this story *our* story. For the first readers, it described their origins, the beginnings of their communities through the work of Paul on this "missionary journey." At the heart of the book the story reaches the reader's heartland. The preface to Luke supports this interpretation by speaking of three levels: the "eyewitnesses [apostles], ministers of the word [Philip, Paul, and others] . . . me," with reference to the third Christian generation and the third missionary wave. The sense of intimacy communicated by the "we" gains impetus from the wealth of local color and narrative detail that contrast the stories of this section with those of chaps. 13–14.

FIRST IN PHILIPPI (16:11-40)

Whereas the narrative of 16:6-7 laconically chronicles the passage of entire provinces, the pace of 16:11-12 slows abruptly with data about daily travel. The first venture in Europe will take place in a little segment of the imperial capital, Philippi, which receives a flattering introduction. Its civic status is a valuable factor for both the outcome of the story and the place of the church in the Roman Empire.

After a swift voyage that itself gave credence to the urgency expressed in the vision, the missionaries settled down for a few days' wait. Finally Sabbath came and with it opportunity to reach out to Jews and their adherents. Lacking a synagogue, the faithful met outdoors by a river. Apparently only women were present, or receptive. Paul persuaded one of these God-fearers, a wealthy merchant from Thyatira named Lydia. She became the leader of a house church after being baptized with her household (cf. v. 40). Lydia was the Cornelius of this new missionary phase. Like other converts, she acted out her faith by providing hospitality. If Paul were to accept her offer, he, too, would be moving in new directions, for never before had he used a gentile home as base. The Lord who had opened her heart (v. 14) also opened his. The barriers between Jew and gentile, female and male, are beginning to dissolve.

Satan did not take all this lying down. Visits to the place of prayer were made unpleasant by an unfortunate woman whose oracular capacity had made her a valuable commodity. She was a slave. Now, however, the power within her recognized the true nature of the missionaries (as many demons had perceived the status of Jesus), and she began to give free advertising. Paul had no use for such vulgar commercial messages. After a few days this began to wear thin, and the vexed evangelist finally silenced her by intoning an exorcism. His diagnosis was correct, and a demon departed, leaving silence in its wake. Thus did the European ministry of Paul open with an exorcism, as had the Galilean ministry of Jesus (Luke 4:31-37), symbolizing the advent of God's reign and the defeat of satanic forces.

Healings and exorcisms often draw awestruck crowds, but not in this particular instance. Rather than praise the goodness of God, the owners of the exorcised slave lamented the loss of income. This was the real motive of their subsequent action. Rather than appear selfish, the owners had Paul and Silas charged with grave crimes, masking their avarice behind the last refuge of scoundrels, seasoned here with a dash of racism and a pinch of old-time religion. Within a flash these base claims produced a crowd to defame the missionaries rather than acclaim the exorcism. Stampeded by the mob, the chief officials had the alleged miscreants viciously whipped and clapped into prison, with stringent instructions for thorough security. The jailer obliged by placing them within stocks in the dark recesses of the innermost chamber of his facilities.

This sudden and drastic calamity did not leave Paul and Silas despondent. Instead of uttering painful groans, they filled the prison air with prayer and hymns of praise, attracting the quiet attention of even their hardened fellow prisoners. Bound for loosing a demon, they worshiped with unfettered souls. Marvelous as this scene is, we are barely given time to contemplate it before it is swept away by an even greater marvel, a quake, accompanied by the opening of the door and the unfastening of chains. Paul, who has shared the fate of Peter and the others, may now share their deliverance. The two are free to leave.

Before reporting this imminent consequence of the quake, Luke draws our attention to the jailer, roused from a sound sleep by the disturbance. He discovers the opened doors and makes the obvious assumption. Rather than be executed for failure to perform his duty, he determines to do away with himself. Just as the sword is poised to plunge into his breast, he hears Paul's reassuring words. With torch in hand this jailer rescued from death by his prisoner rushes into the cell. Casting himself at their feet (cf. 10:25), he utters the one question necessary: "My lords, what can I do to be saved?" He has sensed the presence of the numinous and has turned his thoughts from death to deliverance. By this question the jailer reveals religious sensibilities. Paul and Silas direct him to the real Lord and promise salvation for his entire family. Once the household has assembled, they share their message and receive in turn treatment for their injuries. Paul and Silas had their injuries washed; the jailer and his people received the bath of regeneration. Hospitality naturally follows when they are introduced into his home to celebrate with a meal. This is not explicitly described as a eucharist, but the allusions are plain. Every meal in Luke-Acts has dimensions that intimate the Eucharist.

The arrival of daylight brings a number of intriguing possibilities. How will the city receive the news of the wondrous earthquake? Will the jailer now confront his superiors with his altered views on the characters of those whom he had been directed to secure firmly? Will a trial ensue to examine the fraudulent charges? Not at all. The magistrates have given up the game. They send their official police escort to the jailer, bearing instructions to release Paul and Silas. The motivation for this change of heart is not stated. The jailer is naturally delighted with this wonderful news and rushes to share it with his charges, adding his own pious dismissal to the official discharge. The story has ended happily!

Paul, for his part, will have none of it. Confronting the lictors, he lists official misdeeds, informing them (and us) that he and Silas are Roman citizens. Why have they only now made plain this privileged status, which specifically prohibits punishments such as that which they had endured? In any case, Paul now asserts his rights and even demands a formal cortege. The officials are quite horrified when they hear that they had whipped citizens of Rome and accept the request. Thus the mission to Philippi ends with the solemnity of a Roman procession. Rights and all, the magistrates think it best that the two leave, and they do so, after a pastoral call upon Lydia and the believers in her home.

With this exhilarating story Luke has depicted the epiphany of the Pauline mission to Europe, the triumphant march of the gospel across the Aegean. So fully does the rich and complex plot engage us that we do not easily bring ourselves to question its loose ends and improbable turns. The story is rich in symbol and cross-reference. The initial exorcism evokes memories of Jesus' ministry; by being whipped they share his humiliation also. The prison miracle places Paul and Silas in the company of Peter and the twelve, with one important difference: Paul had no need to escape, for although Roman justice may be administered by craven incompetents, it still holds the prospect of justice. The earthquake and its paraphernalia symbolize rather than effect the release granted by the magistrates. By incorporating within the escape story the tale of the jailer, Luke has also imbedded its interpretation. The jailer brings light (cf. 12:7) into the prison. He is paradoxically the one delivered from sin and rescued from death, reborn in Baptism and saved from disgrace and loss of livelihood. The one who had chained his prisoners in darkness feeds them in light.

The tables are also turned in that the first converts are a named woman and an anonymous man. Each conversion follows the same pattern: proclamation, initiation of an entire household, hospitality. A new community is coming into being. Its nucleus is within house churches. For the first time in Acts the opposition has taken a pagan religio-economic coloring. Those who wish to find in Acts a sympathetic portrait of either paganism or non-Christian Judaism may be disappointed. The same motive of financial loss from the ruin of some crude superstition will emerge at the close of this section, in Ephesus. At our great distance it is easy to observe that Luke's plot often unfolds with all the subtlety of televised professional wrestling matches. Beneath this burlesque surface lies a description of the vanquishing of Satan as embodied in superstition and magic. To us the earthquake looks like magic, but not to Luke. It was a demonstration of the supernatural, to be sure, but Paul did not capitalize upon it for his own benefit; he remained in place to render a service to the jailer. The opened doors of the Philippian jail were doors that admitted gentile believers to the faith. Perhaps this successful encounter with Roman law foreshadows the end of the book and Paul's final vindication. It was certainly a providential circumstance that the first colony of the heavenly city in Europe was planted within this "first" (16:12) city and Roman colony.

MARCHING THROUGH MACEDONIA (17:1-15)

Following this action-packed episode Luke offers two less detailed and less exciting summary reports. Paul will, in fact, work no more reported miracles until the climax in Ephesus. Now that the tone has been set, fifteen verses suffice for the balance of the province, encompassing two missionary sites. Each yields a similar, and familiar, story—with variations.

The road first brings them to Thessalonica, which has a synagogue. Following his custom (and Jesus') Paul attends and is permitted to offer a course of three weekly exegetical sermons with discussion. The Jews proper are generally lukewarm, but many Godfearers agree, including numerous prominent women. The Jews did not take kindly to the loss of their wealthy and influential supporters. In their jealousy they hit upon the notion of riling up a crowd from among the shiftless rabble loitering in the agora. These worthies, in turn, rush upon the house of Jason. The story itself rushes too quickly for us. Who is Jason? The (Jewish?) host of the mission? In any case, they expected to find the missionaries there. Fortunately they were not there. Quickly adjusting their plans, the opponents settle for the reduced booty of Jason and some others, whom they arraign before the magistrates. They claim that Paul and Silas are ecumenical menaces. This is good irony. A base exaggeration at present, it will become increasingly true.

Jason, we now learn, has given shelter to these rascals. To top it off, they claim that all Christians are subversives, a charge the Thessalonian Jews did not originate (Luke 23:2, of Jesus; Acts 24:5, of Paul). The very thought of such sacrilege inflames the patriotic

and law-abiding crowd and worries the officials. We dread their
verdict, but it is rather lenient. They demand bond, which will be
forfeited in the event of more unpleasantness. Since Paul's continued
presence will almost guarantee this, the judgment has the effect of
an expulsion. They slip out of Thessalonica at night, dispatched by
brave followers.

Within a verse Paul is in another synagogue, at Beroea. The Jews
are somewhat more amenable there, daily Bible study leading many
to believe. Among the converts was a large number from the upper
strata. All goes smoothly until, shades of Lystra (14:19-20), the
unrequited Jews of Thessalonica learn of these efforts and arrive to
engage in the usual shenanigans, with the result that Paul must once
more leave. After making various dispositions, Paul departed with
a delegation for Athens. Pagan or Jewish opponents have managed
to create civic unrest in three Macedonian cities and expel Paul from
each. His life has been just as rigorous as 9:15 promised, but the
mission thrives.

A TOUR OF ATHENS (17:16-34)

While briefly marooned in Athens, Paul casts an eye at his famous
surroundings. Like Jesus in the temple (Luke 21:5-6), he is no
admirer of artifacts. He sees idolatry rather than beauty. With that
observation Luke sets the tone for the episode. Idols or not, Paul
will not be idle. He undertakes discussions in both the synagogue
and the agora. Luke uses the same verb for both activities, reminding
us that the early Christians taught like philosophers (cf. 5:12). Dialogue in the Athenian marketplace recalls one of his predecessors,
Socrates, thus establishing a second theme. Christianity is not superstition but *paideia,* cultured learning. That is a third theme.

In the course of these discussions Paul engaged the interests of
adherents of the principal philosophical sects, the Stoics and the
Epicureans. Like the crowd at Jerusalem (2:12), their reactions are
mixed. Some regard him as a philosophical dilettante. Others suspect
that he is introducing new gods. That is an old charge at Athens.
Socrates died for violating it. When Paul, like Socrates, is brought
before the court of the Areopagus, suspense mounts. Will he, too,

be condemned? Yet there is also the excitement of seeing the Christian hero deliver his message to this distinguished body. How will he fare? At this point Luke slips us a hint with a rare intervention, reminding the reader of the notoriously fickle and superficial nature of the Athenians. Little can be expected from the likes of them.

Paul still gives it his best shot, an apposite, witty, and well-constructed address. Opening with the classical salutation, "Men of Athens," itself a reminder of all those famous orations read in school, Paul flatters the audience with a reference to the piety exhibited in their monuments. This is a nice touch, meeting for the dramatic audience the requirements of an initial compliment, while striking readers as a dig at superstition. We continue to smile as he recounts his tourist ramblings, remembering v. 16. In the course of them, he recounts, he came upon an inscription "to an unknown god." This will serve him as object lesson and text. Beginning where the audience is theologically, Paul has a notion he can exploit for three ends: as a confession of religious longing paganism cannot satisfy, as a tacit confession of that ignorance of God that will place gentile pagans on a level with Jerusalem Jews, and as evidence that his faith is not novel.

With Jews Paul argued from Scripture as a source for the revelation of God. To these pagans he must expound the god they revere in ignorance as the creator of all and begetter of the one person from whom all others are descended. This notion of the essential unity of the human race is both the justification of a world mission and the basis for its accomplishment. For Acts, Paul is the figure who embodies within his diverse backgrounds and cultural accomplishments this unity. All people, Paul claims, belong to the God who has created places to dwell and periods of time (= eras of salvation history). Creation reveals an innate quest for the source of being. To prove that all descend from God, Paul quotes a pagan poet as he elsewhere cites Scripture (for the idea, see Luke 3:38). Anthropology provides a critique of idolatry. Ignorance, previously overlooked, is no longer an excuse, for the same God who made all from one will judge all upon one basis, through one agent, who rose from the dead to demonstrate this.

As before and later, the notion of resurrection proves to be the stumbling block, although some preserve open minds and Paul leaves without interference, having converted at least one member of that distinguished body and a woman of undisclosed status. So concludes this silver-tongued oration in a golden old classical setting. In the end, the reaction of the cultured Athenians had much in common with that of the later Sanhedrin (23:6-12), with a divided audience, two sects, resurrection as principal issue, and the use of a clever device. In the case of the Areopagus, of course, there was no more than a hint of danger. With the Sanhedrin it will be different.

From this attractive episode Luke's readers could take comfort in realizing that even Paul at his most brilliant did not sway many philosophers. They should not despair at the meager reapings their own efforts brought. There is more pleasure than consolation within these eighteen verses. They include not only the most famous of all Lukan speeches, but, through the deft application of surprisingly few touches, a portrait of remarkable vividness and color. The apparently haphazard potpourri of allusions to well-known Athenian qualities and things coalesces into a coherent picture, which complements the speech and leaves an impression that alleviates the obvious lack of major success.

SOJOURN IN CORINTH (18:1-17)

Upon arriving in the bustling and booming Roman colony of Corinth, Paul comes upon a Jewish couple, Aquila and Priscilla, whom the emperor had expelled from Rome. The elaborate introduction of this pair piques our curiosity. Rather than describe their role, Luke turns to Aquila's profession, or rather, trade. Paul takes up residence with them because he is in the same line of work. This is something of a shock, for, whether as persecutor or as missionary, Paul has always seemed to devote his full time to religion. Nor does manual labor seem congruent with his status. (At 20:34 we shall learn more about this.) After this announcement about work and living arrangements, Aquila and Priscilla disappear from the story for some time. Luke does not even state that they were Christians.

On the Sabbath, Paul labored to convert Jews and Greeks. With the arrival of Silas and Timothy (who apparently brought money), he could devote more time to missionary work. This stepped-up pace generated the usual opposition, finally issuing in the ritual declaration of separation from the synagogue. Paul transferred his base to the home of a God-fearer, Titius Justus. Luke then reports a real coup, the accession of the probably wealthy Crispus, a leader of the synagogue, together with his people. Even after leaving the synagogue, Paul strove to convert other Jews. At this exultant moment, Paul receives a vision, beginning with the traditional "Do not be afraid." Afraid of what? Conventional or not, it alarms us. The vision fills Paul with courage needed to sustain him in the face of some great danger and also helps to explain why he remained so long in Corinth. This revelation makes the importance of the Corinthian mission indisputable. Thus fortified, Paul works there for eighteen months.

This gave Paul's enemies a good deal to oppose and considerable time to seek an opportunity for mischief. With the arrival of a new governor, Gallio, they believe their deliverance is at hand. The Jews whisk Paul into court alleging, "This man is persuading people to worship God contrary to the law." The ambiguity of their language, which omits reference to the source of the law in question, is a clumsy attempt at cleverness, easily sidestepped by Gallio. Before Paul can begin to formulate a defense, Gallio replies, in words quoted by Luke, that no heinous crime is in question, merely disputes about Jewish legal trivia, concerning which he has no curiosity. After Gallio rudely dismisses the plaintiffs, those present promptly administer a beating to the synagogue leader Sosthenes. Gallio still does not care. Sosthenes is the latest in a series of would-be persecutors to taste his own medicine.

Luke thus blithely portrays the beating that Judaism took at Corinth. Moreover, the indifference of Rome to these religious issues is reassuring. Paul has confronted two Roman governors. The first was interested in his message and was converted. The second was not interested and saw no reason to bother. This growing movement is no threat to Roman law and order. Although Luke is not done with the matter, this will do for now. Paul's work at Corinth thus ends with the triumph of legal vindication. Readers have by now had opportunity to detect a pattern of proclamation, success, opposition, and vindication. Paul has not yet faced any sustained legal action. Nonetheless, he has usually left town shortly after encountering justice or allegations by a raging mob.

PILGRIMAGE AND RETURN (18:18—19:7)

Paul is in no more of a hurry to leave Corinth than other cities. Bidding the congregation *adieu,* he sails for Syria, together with Priscilla and Aquila, whose names appear to frame the narrative. Priscilla now appears in first place, a change of position comparable to the inversion of the names of Paul and Barnabas in chap. 13. Before leaving the southern port of Corinth, Paul shaves his head in accordance with a vow, leaving no doubt of his continuing loyalty to the temple. The pious deed also places time constraints upon him.

Thus he must hastily deposit Priscilla and Aquila in the great Asian metropolis of Ephesus, having time for only a brief visit to whet the appetite of the synagogue congregation—and the readers. Promising to return, God willing, Paul journeyed on south to Caesarea, paid his visit to Jerusalem, and then headed back north, stopping at Antioch, where he is, of course, still welcome. After that comes a series of briefly noted pastoral visits by an overland route that will, in due time, return him to Ephesus. The journey repeats that of 15:41—16:7. These summaries assure the reader that, his new successes and Jewish opposition notwithstanding, Paul remains bound by friendship to Antioch and Jerusalem. As usual, these summaries also prepare for a transition and highlight what follows.

While Paul is engaged in these matters, Luke takes the spotlight from him for a rare moment at 18:24 and looks back to Ephesus in time to witness the arrival of one Apollos of Alexandria. This worthy receives a most impressive and elaborate introduction, climaxing with the unexpected statement that he knew of John's baptism alone. When Apollos took up a preaching mission in the synagogue, Priscilla and Aquila, being in attendance, heard Apollos and took steps to correct his deficient knowledge of the tradition. The believers in

Ephesus—there were some—approve of his plans to visit Greece
and supply him with a letter of introduction. There Apollos became
a formidable adversary of the Jews and a great boon to the Christians.
Having established Apollos as a Pauline disciple once removed, the
couple have made their one contribution to Acts.

When, at long last, Paul returns to Ephesus, he happens upon
some disciples. Christians, we presume. A check of their credentials,
however, reveals that they, who follow John, have never even heard
of the Holy Spirit! Do they represent a residue of Apollos's pre-
Priscilla period? Probably not, for the issue in their case is a lack
of the sacramentally mediated experiential gift. Paul does, however,
point out the proper place of John in salvation history and then
completes their initiation, leading to reception of the Spirit. Peter
and John had done much the same for the "heretical" Jews of
Samaria (8:14-25). Luke gives the statistics at the end, a practice
of which he is fond. Twelve is a good number.

TRIUMPH IN EPHESUS (19:8-40)

Paul now resumes his accustomed style, returning to the synagogue he had briefly visited in 18:19. The pattern runs its course
for the final time. On this occasion three months pass before Paul
withdraws his followers and moves to the hall of Tyrannus, where
evangelistic instruction takes place upon a daily basis. For two years
his labors continue, until the word has radiated throughout the province. When Luke reached the climax of his description of the apostolic ministry in Jerusalem, he spoke of extraordinary wonders
(5:12-16). The same means serve to demonstrate the success of
Paul's activity in Ephesus. Even cast-off handkerchieves accomplished healings and exorcisms.

An amusing incident follows. Paul's success had depressed the
local market for exorcism. Competitive pressures led some to adopt
the names of Jesus and Paul. Among the practitioners of this up-
to-date approach were seven scions of one Sceva, a Jewish high
priest. In the example provided the demon was not fooled. Ac-
knowledging Jesus and Paul, it demanded their names—a frequent
demonic ploy. Then, without awaiting a reply, it assaulted them

through its medium, leaving the priestly pair with battered bodies and tattered clothes, compelled to flee in disgrace. Thus the would-be exorcists terminated a house call looking more like their patients than like masters over demons (cf. Mark 5:1-20).

Word of this coup spread, leading to a mass conversion of Jews and gentiles, many of whom now came forward to confess their practice of magical arts (for which Ephesus was famous). Fearing more boomerangs, a vast throng cast magical papyri upon a public bonfire. The closing statistical note states that this rubbish had a market value of about $1,000,000. That is power.

Now at the peak of his success, Paul receives a revelation directing him westward. After visits to Macedonia, Greece, and Jerusalem, he "must see Rome." The element of necessity echoes Jesus' predictions of his passion. Just as Jerusalem was Jesus' goal, Rome will be Paul's. The reader cannot help but feel alarm. Dispatching two of his assistants for some advance work (cf. Luke 9:51-52), Paul lingers a bit longer in the city he has determined to leave.

Both Jews and gentiles have broken with their religious pasts, the former by leaving the synagogue, the latter by abandoning magic. The value of Jewish exorcisms has declined considerably. Crushing as these setbacks were, they do not mean extinction. Paganism will speak first.

Before recording Paul's departure, Luke introduces an interlude. The camera focuses upon one Demetrius, a manufacturer of silver models of the famous temple of Artemis of Ephesus. Gathering the craftsmen whose livelihood depended upon the piety of tourists and devotees, Demetrius delivers a stem-winding speech, reminding them of the source of their daily bread, which is now in grave jeopardy. Paul's polemic against idolatry is ruining the tourist trade. This unfriendly witness thus confirms the observation of 19:10. Onto the logs of impending unemployment, Demetrius hurls the brands of piety, exhorting the silversmiths to protect the threatened esteem of their world-famous patron, Artemis.

Galvanized by the prospect of this double insult, the silversmiths begin their ritual shout: "Great is Artemis of the Ephesians!" Their outrage sets the city ablaze. The whole populace sprints to the theater for a community assembly, with two of Paul's colleagues, Gaius and Aristarchus, in tow. What of Paul himself? His intention to enter the theater and still the riot was resisted by anxious believers, to whom the Asiarchs, some of whom were Paul's friends and feared for his safety, added their voice. The depth of their regard is apparent in their willingness to communicate with Paul in the crisis of grave civic tumult. So Paul stayed home.

Meanwhile, chaos reigned in the theater. The assembly was in shambles, with everyone talking and no one having accurate information. By v. 33 the reader is also caught up in this maelstrom. An effort sponsored by the Jews to have one Alexander speak was shouted down when his identity became known. We shall thus never know whether he wished to disassociate the Jews from these Christians or denounce the new movement. All the crowd can do is resume its ritual cultic chant. For two hours the place reverberates with their cry "Great is Artemis of the Ephesians." Paganism may speak with one voice, but it is no more than the racket of a mindless rabble easily brought to a frenzy through the machinations of greedy craftsmen.

Artemis does not respond, but the government does. Before this disturbance yields to violence, the chief official rises to play a part already immortalized by Gamaliel. Reminding the people of their incontrovertible status, he proceeds to vindicate and acquit the Christians. There exist proper legal and political channels for any legitimate complaints Demetrius and his ilk may have. The Secretary General of the Ephesian assembly knows what is going on. If Christians and pagans wish to fight, let them do so in court. "There are proconsuls." Yes, there are, and Roman governors tend to take a dim view of this kind of participatory democracy. Cities plagued by riot are liable to lose, not enhance, their vaunted privileges. The "assembly" (ekklēsia) is therewith dismissed. On that note Luke drops the curtain upon Paul's Ephesian mission.

Acts 19 is justly famous. In a series of gripping episodes, each complete and vivid, and all forming a coherent plot, Luke portrays the climax of Paul's work as a missionary. The victories have been as numerous and important as the story is varied and exciting. Heresy and sect give way in the face of sound instruction and legitimate ministry. Jews and gentiles alike join in throngs. The line between

Christian miracles and pagan magic is sharply drawn. Wounded pagans lash out with a hapless incantation, achieving no more than the danger of Roman intervention.

As the public activity of Paul draws to a close, issues of Luke's own era begin to loom on the horizon. Heresy, syncretism, Jewish-Christian relations, questions of church and state, and behavior toward pagans were matters of immediate concern to Luke's audience. Lessons could be learned from this account of their solution at Ephesus.

Scarcely less evident is the defense of Christianity. Luke does not attempt to place rivals in the best light. His contrasts are strong. The opposition is of the basest sort and possesses the worst of motives. Friends are better placed, including the leading official, who has pronounced Paul innocent of crimes against the state or disrespect of established religion. The Asiarchs, men of the highest standing, have taken a vigorous interest in protecting Paul from danger.

Money rattles throughout the chapter, from the fees of itinerant charlatans and the cost of magical books to the naked greed (slightly veiled with piety) of the silversmiths. Acts 20:34 will illuminate this concern. In this portrayal of the culmination of Paul's Aegean ministry, Luke draws together the culmination of many of his leading themes.

The movement cares for itself. Paul is effectively out of the picture after 19:11. He need do nothing to immobilize the sons of Sceva. The conflagration of magical papyri was an act of spontaneous repentance. Demetrius could invoke the dread name of Paul, but the riot started on his account was extinguished by the leading civic official, who said no less than what Paul would have presented as his own defense. Artemis digs her own grave. All these opponents were put out of business without the need for Paul to utter a word. This portrait testifies to his immense power and also suggests that the church can endure after his death by following his lead. Paul's hand (cf. v. 11), like the hand of God, is invisibly present.

SUMMARY

Thus with the warrant and blessing of Jerusalem, a flock of gentile believers has been formed, joined nearly everywhere by believing

Jews, for Paul has not in any way abandoned either his ancestral faith or his obligation to preach first in the synagogue. The story of his work has become an ode to joy mingled with the tragedy of so much Jewish rejection. The voyage of the gospel across and about the Aegean has not always been smooth, but progress has been constant. The storms of opposition have not submerged the little bark of the church. The most fearsome opponents are jealous Jews, who are perfectly satisfied when they can get Christians in trouble with civic powers or Roman officials, thus identifying themselves ultimately with pagans, whose motives and tactics do not greatly differ. The similarly motivated efforts of the latter frame this section of Acts, in Philippi and Ephesus. Both close with complete legal vindication. These must have been matters of some concern to Luke.

Acts 19:21 announces a new journey, one of many in Acts. The language suggests, however, that this one will be different. Paul sets out for Rome just as Jesus had set out for Jerusalem. Having shared the success of his master, the missionary now seems to be embarking on a parallel path toward his destiny.

5

Unfettered to the End

20:1—28:30

Under the shadow of 19:21-22, the victorious Paul begins preparations for his journey, which is to open with pastoral visits to Macedonia and Greece, followed by a stop at Jerusalem, and then on to Rome, the center of the empire and the end of his earthly labors. Missionary outreach is no longer the subject of Acts. Paul and his ultimate fate, clearly alluded to but not described, are the subject of this final section. The account will entangle Paul (and the reader) in legal issues. Paul spends most of this section in chains and many aspects of his own life seem to duplicate elements of Jesus' passion. The story is by no means less interesting than hitherto, and readers will find it difficult to detach themselves from the stirring narrative to inquire about its purpose.

A FATEFUL JOURNEY (19:21—20:16)

In accordance with his plans, Paul sets out for Macedonia, after appropriate ministrations and farewells. Only a short summary of this lengthy expedition is available (20:1-2). Then the specter of a plot by unbelieving Jews intervenes. These enemies have not retired from the field. This conspiracy required a change of travel plans. So Paul sets out by another route for the holy city, surrounded by an entourage of named companions. Their number amounts to the sacred figure of seven. The list is once again a form of solemn punctuation—a harbinger of new things. At Philippi the "we" returns. "We" had last spoken in the same place (16:17). The specific details of the journey add a drumbeat to accompany the journey, pacing off the days and stops on the way to destiny, raising suspense with their gripping verisimilitude and somewhat ominous monotony.

The procession halts at Troas for a sample of Paul's pastoral activity. On Sunday he celebrates the Eucharist and preaches to a house church assembled in the third story of an urban tenement. This homiletical conversation went on and on, until midnight. Lamps added light, heat, smoke, and perhaps symbol. Possibly for a breath of fresh air, or maybe to hear and see better, an unfortunate young man named Eutychus ("Lucky") had perched himself in a window. As the service went on, he fell asleep, bringing a smile to the face of all who have ever dozed off during a long sermon. Such smiles quickly vanish in horror as we hear that he plunged to his death from the window. Paul stopped his teaching to attend to the matter, embracing the body (cf. 1 Kings 17:21-24; Luke 4:24-27), and offering reassurance. Then, as if nothing untoward had happened, Paul returned to his task and we are pulled back into the service until its eventual conclusion at dawn. Only then, almost as an afterthought, do we learn that Eutychus had been fortunate after all.

Like Peter (Acts 9:38-41) and Jesus (Luke 7:11-17), Paul has revived a corpse. It is not insignificant that this event falls within a section gradually taking the shape of a passion narrative. Resurrection defeats the forces of death. The eucharistic frame (vv. 7, 11) points to the locus of miracles within the church of Luke's era and explicates the sacrament as the celebration of risen life.

After this vivid and exciting incident, the itinerary resumes with a wealth of specifics, slowing the action to a nearly unbearable pace. Intent upon arriving by Pentecost, the party bypasses Ephesus. This is the second reference to the Jewish calendar, an indication of continuity. They did halt at Miletus. While there, Paul summoned the presbyters of Ephesus. When they arrive it emerges that Paul has something to say to these leaders.

THE TESTAMENT OF PAUL (20:17-35)

What Paul has to say, ancient readers would have realized, takes the form of the final address made to family or followers by a dying worthy. The speech thus foreshadows and presumes Paul's death. In the manner of such orations, the speech makes full use of personal example as a basis for exhortation. This sermon also exhibits a number of themes found in Jesus' final message to his disciples (Luke 22:14-38), thereby enhancing the similarity of their Passions. The pastoral model set forth here mirrors a rather different image of Paul than has appeared in earlier chapters, but Luke has given enough hints to make it palatable. Blood, sweat, and tears characterize Paul's labors. Pathos colors the speech and lends it power.

Like other farewell addresses, this sermon is a testament, addressed to all believers everywhere. In it Luke lifts for a moment the veil concealing the church of his own day. The problems described are those faced by later Christians. Paul offers himself as a model for the clergy. Their priorities are (1) to care for themselves, and (2) to care for the flocks over which they are placed (cf. Luke 12:32). The metaphor of "shepherd" was commonly used of leaders in the ancient world. As shepherds (called both "presbyters/elders" and "bishops") they are to see that their charges receive nurture and avoid seeking personal gain. Money and leadership are regularly linked in Luke-Acts (cf. Luke 12:35-40, 16; 17:7-10; 18:18-30). Shepherds will confront wolves (i.e., false teachers) who will strike when Paul is no longer in charge of the household. These heretics may be refuted by his teaching. Paul publicly taught all that is of real value. The speech suggests that heretics will appeal to a secret teaching devoid of value for daily life.

Within this paradigm for ministry lies a defense of Paul's own conduct. Apparently he was alleged to have sponged from his congregations and to have stimulated esoteric speculation (cf. 1 and 2 Corinthians). To the readers of Acts such charges are outrageous calumnies. The speech further exonerates Paul from later problems. By supporting not only himself but also his colleagues (v. 34), Paul has preached a lifelong sermon against clerical avarice.

In the light of the Milesian address Paul shines forth as a man of sorrows, laboring to fulfill his mission while earning his daily bread by the sweat of his brow. Hints of later difficulties can also be glimpsed. Verse 23 generates suspense, foreshadowing his reception at Jerusalem. In the next verse mystery recedes without lessening tension. This is the first of three "passion predictions" (20:23-25; 21:4, 11-13) revealing the destiny Paul will share with Jesus.

Following an exhortation to almsgiving and a closing prayer, the scene dissolves in an outpouring of grief, sorrow felt also by the reader. On this poignant note Luke pulls the curtain upon his solitary example of hortatory Christian proclamation. Through the one representative scene of 20:7-12 and this presumably typical speech, he has forged an unforgettable portrait of Paul as pastor in word and act. Together these two units constitute a sort of "last supper" comparable to that of Jesus. The reader also feels considerable apprehension about what is coming next.

ALLEGATIONS OF APOSTASY (21:1-26)

The journey resumes and the numerous travel details slow the pace and heighten suspense. Many communities show their support for Paul, adding their witness to the extent of his contribution. Tyre requires a halt to unload the ship. During this hiatus more prophecies of great danger occur. The Spirit may warn of danger, but this does not override the injunction to Paul. Another tearful farewell on the beach concludes this interlude, made even more tender by the presence of women and children.

At Caesarea they stay with Philip, who lives there with four unmarried daughters endowed with prophetic gifts. The promise of Pentecost is still being fulfilled (2:17). None of their prophecies are recorded. Instead, after some days, Agabus of Jerusalem appears. Disparate elements of the story of Acts lodge together: Jerusalem, the Seven, and Paul. During the course of his visit Agabus delivers the most dramatic and explicit of the passion predictions, demonstrating with Paul's belt that he will be bound in Jerusalem. His words recall Luke 18:32. In response to this vivid and dire warning all, including "we," raise their voices and plead with Paul not to go. He stands resolute in this his own Garden of Gethsemane (Luke 22:33-42). He will not flee, as had the disciples, but like Jesus he will go forth to meet his fate. If necessary he, too, will die in Jerusalem. The followers then state their own resolve to be disciples, echoing Jesus' own prayer, "Your will be done." Suspense continues to mount. Will he actually die in Jerusalem? What has happened that makes this journey so threatening for Paul, who has freely and recently visited the city?

Still, days go by, with increasing tension, until they finally prepare to make their way toward Jerusalem, accompanied by believers from Caesarea, who escort them to their lodgings in the home of another old disciple, Mnason of Cyprus. Even in Jerusalem there are many links with the gentile mission. If it is safe for Mnason, it can be safe for Paul. The following day Paul reports to James, the leader of the church, who receives him warmly with a surrounding group of presbyters. As in chap. 15, they listen in awe to Paul's report. He has no monopoly on good news, however, for they have accomplishments of their own to share: hosts of believers in Jesus who stand firm in the observance of Torah. Yet the glad advent of these believers who have not compromised a jot or tittle of their devotion has raised a small problem. They have been told the most dreadful things about Paul, who is said to teach apostasy to Diaspora Jews. We who have read of the circumcision of Timothy and innumerable reminders of Paul's piety are outraged, but there it is. James evidently regards this as Paul's problem, for which a solution is at hand. James directs Paul to pay the expenses of four (poor?) Christians bound by a vow and to purify himself with them, thus deflating any basis for criticism. James makes it clear that this represents no shift in the gentile requirements imposed in chap. 15. Acts 21:18-26 formally summarizes the missions to gentiles and Jews. The former are not bound to observe Torah; the latter, including Paul, are.

It goes without saying that Paul, who has undertaken vows on his own, will oblige them in this matter. The only drawback is that his visit cannot be so brief or private as planned. The ritual procedure requires a week, granting time for the agents of malice to implement their wicked schemes. Still, all goes well on the first day, and the second, and the day thereafter, until at long last the seventh day comes. We may begin to breathe a bit more easily. Despite all the grim warnings and gloomy prognostications, Paul seems to be out of the woods.

A PLAN BACKFIRES (21:27-40)

For the seventh and final time Paul goes to the temple, where
. . . the scheme backfires. Rather than convince others of his piety,
his presence exposes him to the eyes of some fault-finding Asian
Jews. His success had led to his undoing. Evidently life in Ephesus
had instructed them in the fine art of fomenting riots. They rouse
the crowd, raising against Paul the charges once laid against Stephen,
adding the inflammatory charge that he has shared these blasphemies
with the whole world. To cap these iniquities Paul is accused of
introducing gentiles into the temple he attacks. (Luke intervenes to
advise that this was an error rather than a lie. Both intervention and
excuse are unusual for him.) Whatever its basis, that accusation
works like a lighted match in a tub of gasoline. Both city and temple
erupt. Dragging Paul out of the sanctuary (lest his blood defile the
premises; cf. 14:19-20), they slam the gates and get ready for a
lynching. Word of these proceedings reaches the commander of the
Roman garrison, who intervenes quickly at the head of a large
detachment. The appearance of these soldiers halts the crowd before
it can finish its pious endeavor. The commanding tribune has Paul
taken and chained, and then asks his name and offense. So many,
varied, and simultaneous are the replies that he quickly abandons
this first of several attempts to uncover the facts. In the category
of riots, Jerusalem need concede nothing to Ephesus. The prisoner
is to be hauled up to the fortress, where torture awaits.

So battered was Paul that he could not negotiate the steps in his
manacles and had to be carried by soldiers, to the accompaniment
of bloodthirsty shouts from the frustrated crowd. Rather than repent
of their crime in demanding Jesus' death, the people of Jerusalem
are repeating it. On the very verge of the doors of torture and
confinement, Paul politely requested permission to speak. He had
no more than opened his mouth than the tribune realized that he
was a gentleman. This provoked an astonished inquiry, explaining
at length his initial impression that Paul was an insurgent leader.
The tribune thereby displays his political innocence, for guerrillas
were more likely to initiate a lynching than experience one. The
mistaken identity became a perfect foil for Paul's famous response.

He *is* a Jew (thus he was lawfully in the sanctuary), and also a
citizen of a famous enclave of Hellenic culture. We learn of this
high status when the tribune does, for Paul has reserved this revelation for the moment when it will do him the most good. Through
it he regains the initiative and quickly receives permission to deliver
a public address.

Somehow the Tarsian, wounded in body but not in spirit or pride,
summoned up the resources (cf. 14:19-20) to mount the very steps
over which he had recently been carried and, with the forceful
presence of a born leader, to still the howling mob. Paul thus joins
Jesus and Peter by speaking in the temple. Having demonstrated to
the tribune his Hellenic erudition, he will now display his ability at
Semitic oratory.

REVELATION IN THE TEMPLE (22:1-29)

This speech is called a "defense." Defense of Paul has, in fact,
been a leading subject since 19:21. It will dominate the rest of the
book. Acts 20:18-35 permitted Paul to respond to allegations made
by later Christians. Now he will speak to Jews, continuing that
defense which began with his arrival in Jerusalem. Beneath this
speech lies a fundamental irony: Paul, while engaged in purification,
faces charges of defilement. As the reader knows how false the
charges are, the speech ignores them. Its entire tenor renders them
unthinkable.

Opening with the same respectful address invoked by Stephen,
Paul sets forth unimpeachable Jewish credentials cemented by commendable zeal. We, with the audience, learn that Paul had been
reared in Jerusalem and schooled by Gamaliel. In accord with his
conviction and zeal, Paul assumed the role of persecutor.

Implicit within the subsequent reprise of his Damascus experience
is a critique of such zeal, an example of which occurred in vv. 6-
16. Through this second rendition of Paul's "conversion," Luke is
beginning to reshape our understanding of it. Ananias recedes to
the status of a pious Jewish observer of God's plan. The title "witness" brings Paul as close to the apostolic circle (Luke 24:48) as
Luke can take him. There is no mention of the punitive blinding.

No longer does Paul's commission come from his conversation with Ananias in Damascus. Instead there is a most dramatic and apposite environment for this pivotal event. Rapt, like Isaiah (Isa. 6:1-9), in ecstasy in the temple, Paul also sees the Lord and hears a command to depart. In accordance with the customs applying to calls, Paul objects. The following reference to Stephen and Paul's role in his death shows that the irony and edge of his speech are becoming sharper. God repeats the command, with explanation— Paul is being sent far off (2:39) to the Gentiles.

That hated word rekindles the crowd. The thought of Gentiles sharing in their blessings is odious. Faced with renewed violence, the tribune reverts to square one, the use of torture. His subordinates will attend to the details. So Paul is once again humiliated, stripped naked, and tied with outstretched limbs ready for the lash. As the first blow was about to fall, Paul raised a technical point: "Is it lawful to whip a Roman citizen who has not been condemned?" Chapter 16 has taught us the answer to this question, and we cannot understand how Paul has so patiently waited to the last possible moment before playing his trump card. So convincing was his manner that they did not challenge his status but withdrew while the centurion in charge went to confront angrily his superior. The latter hastened to the scene and asked if it were really true. It was. Perhaps still dubious, the tribune noted that his own acquisition of the franchise had been costly. Paul observed that *his* citizenship came from birth. Hearing this, the soldiers leapt back as if in the vicinity of the numinous. To these auxiliary soldiers Roman citizens were like divine beings. The tribune can only hope that his mistreatment of a prestigious citizen will not be detected.

The action alternates between legal difficulties and religious controversy until the two become one. Paul is well equipped by education, status, and experience to deal with challenges on both these fronts. With even a modicum of justice, he should prevail. James and the four are available as witnesses; no evidence that he introduced gentiles can be produced; the Romans hold him. They are not the temple police. Romans demand evidence.

DISCOVERING THE FACTS (22:30—23:11)

This demand motivates the tribune to release Paul from his chains the next day and summon the Sanhedrin (who evidently meet at his request) into session. Although his intentions are the best, he has unwittingly led Paul into a trap, placing him at the disposal of the same body that had savagely murdered Stephen without a sentence. No speech by Gamaliel will save this day.

The scene has two parallel sections to reinforce its point. In 22:30—23:5 Paul is pitted against the high priest. In 23:6-10 the leading parties clash. In each segment Paul seizes the initiative and throws the opposition off balance. By this courage and resourcefulness Paul keeps the wolves at bay until the tribune intervenes. There is suspense for readers, because we know what the Sanhedrin is capable of, while the tribune does not.

Boldly seizing the floor, Paul quickly summarizes the biography he has recently given and throws down the gauntlet. The Sanhedrin has no grounds for wishing him dead. Unable to refute this claim, Ananias resorts to having some lackey administer a brutal slap. Undaunted, Paul taunts his tormentor with an elegant prophecy of his death (he was assassinated in the year 66), together with a protest against both the proceedings and the blow. Reproached for disrespect, Paul claims that he did not know whom he had insulted, and cites the relevant Scripture passage regarding the honor due high priests. He has his cake and has eaten it too, for who could imagine that such a bully and cad was the high priest?

Now Paul turns to the council. Knowing its partisan shibboleths, he appeals to the Pharisees to rally to his side. They do, and the stately tribunal degenerates into roughhouse brawlers. Lest Paul be dismembered in the turmoil, the tribune asserts his authority and returns him to custody. Our admiration for Paul's legal acumen and fortitude have grown. One cannot say the same about the Sanhedrin, for it is little different from the Jerusalem rabble. As often, the doctrine of the resurrection is the leading point at issue. This is no cause for Roman intervention.

In the wake of these pulsing episodes of violence followed by Roman "rescue," Paul receives a comforting vision that explains his trials. They will be occasions for witness in both Jerusalem and Rome. As always, such visions bring no less alarm than consolation to the reader. What will happen now? The Sanhedrin may be in a shambles, but its members can quickly regroup. They and their friends are not willing to let Paul linger in Roman custody. The vision does make it evident, however, that behind these machinations and blows of fate lurks the hand of God.

A FAST ESCAPE (23:12-35)

By dawn of the next day these opponents were already hard at work, nourishing themselves with a solemn oath to abstain from both food and drink until Paul was killed. This pledge puts into motion the most elaborately narrated of all the plots against the hero. Its context deserves consideration.

Like chaps. 4–7, Acts 23:12—26:32 presents three cycles based upon recurrent elements variously presented. These elements include some action against Paul, which is thwarted; hearings or "trials" before a Roman governor (composed of summaries or statements by both prosecution and defense), an official "verdict" of sorts; and gubernatorial shortcomings. Each cycle stresses one of the elements. The final segment, in chap. 26, consists of argument and verdict alone.

In the first sequence the conspirators, who number in excess of forty desperate men, approach the leaders of the Sanhedrin, repeat their oath, and reveal the plan. If the leaders will make representations to the tribune that they wish Paul returned to them for further examination, the conspirators will kill him in transport. This plot cleverly plays to the tribune's deeply felt desire to ascertain the facts. Determined fanatics have devised a frightening scheme with every prospect of success. Providence, however, sprang a leak in their security. Paul, it appears, has a nephew who gets word of the plan and visits the prison to inform his uncle. He, in turn, orders an available centurion to convey the lad to the commander. This the centurion does, as we see and hear. Sensitively escorting the young man to a private spot, the tribune interrogates him. Encouraged by these considerations, which also touch the readers' sentiments, the

youth reports what he knows. Tomorrow, we learn, is the day fixed
for the ambush. There is no time to lose. All they lack to fulfill
their ambitions, ratified by a dreadful oath now described for the
third time, is the innocent cooperation of the gullible tribune.

After his informant pledges silence, the tribune quickly reveals
that he is no less skilled at tactical planning than at intelligence
gathering. Summoning two subordinates, he dictates orders to one
and a communication to the other. Since the ambush is planned for
the morrow, they will move at once. A nocturnal operation offers
greater secrecy. Two hundred regular infantry, seventy horse, and
two hundred other arms will comprise the task force. This disposition
is risky, for it will leave the urban garrison dangerously small. Paul's
safety justifies the risk, however, and so ardent are his opponents
that they might overwhelm a smaller force. By these arrangements
the importance of Paul emerges through the clouds of arrest. The
object of the detachment is to deliver Paul safe and sound to the
governor. The tribune, Lysias, dashes off a clever note to his superior
Felix, the governor. Fortunately, we can read this letter and smile
at the tribune's self-exculpation. Moreover, the notion that Paul had
been arrested by Jews and rescued by Romans has been sown. This
will turn out to be Lysias's only opportunity to evaluate Paul's guilt.
He takes it. Paul, in Lysias's eyes, is innocent of any great offense.

The combination of superior force, speed, and daring paid off.
When the expedition had reached Antipatris by nightfall, they had
cleared the zone of gravest danger. The infantry were returned to
the garrison as the cavalry alone could safely take Paul to Caesarea.
The governor accepted their prisoner, perused Lysias's memo, and
inquired after Paul's province of origin. These routine items introduce a link with the Jesus tradition (Luke 23:6-7) and the possibility
that Paul will be remanded to the governor of Cilicia. The further
this business gets from Jerusalem, the better for Paul. Any incipient
hope quickly evaporates when Felix promises a hearing upon the
arrival of the complainants. Still, Caesarea is more salubrious than
Jerusalem, and probably any procurator would be more favorable
toward Paul than some unprincipled high priest. Paul thus enters
this new custody with some grounds for hope. He has escaped a
truly diabolical and well-concocted plot.

As they await the forthcoming trial, those so inclined may feast their minds upon the situation of the thwarted plotters, whose iron-clad oath has thrice been reported. How will these scrupulous zealots now fare, impaled upon the dilemma of conscience and biological necessity? Presumably the latter will triumph, as one by one they secretly betray their solemn conjuration. The equally attractive alternative is good riddance. They should have listened to Gamaliel.

A BATTLE OF WORDS (24:1-23)

Justice will not long delay, for after five days the accusers appear, presumably upon orders. Among them, surprisingly, is the high priest, Ananias, who regarded the matter as so important that he left Jerusalem. We hear nothing of witnesses from the temple or of Lysias. The Jewish leaders have brought along a barrister, Tertullus, securing for the prosecution the professional help of a Greek orator, who will be handy at persuading a governor. Paul will represent himself. This allows us to see him go head-to-head with a master of the Greek art of rhetoric in an oratorical duel.

Tertullus opens with a conventional bit of flattery laden with the religio-political terms of the day: "peace," "providence," "thanks-giving." They are also important terms in Luke-Acts. If true, they give cause for hope. If false, they create a basis for irony. In order to keep his promise of brevity, Tertullus must reduce his accusations to the basics, all of which are lies. In the traditional style, he hurls reckless epithets. Paul is an international agitator whose teaching breeds a plague of riots. This contentious creature is the ringleader of the despicable Nazarene sect. The charges infuriate readers who know that Paul has been the constant *victim* of agitators. Still, they testify to his importance. Paul, not James, not the apostles, is the leading figure of the movement. The Jewish authorities, Tertullus claims, apprehended him in the very act of seeking to defile the temple. Again, this strikes us as more than a bit unfair. Mobs are not authorities, and Paul had attempted nothing of the sort. Satisfied with this brisk summary, Tertullus offers to let the accused condemn himself. His clients applauded his wisdom and added their affirmations.

Paul is equal to this challenge. After expressing confidence in his judge, he smashes the ball Tertullus has floated into his court (vv. 11-12). Restricting his defense to the matter in question, Paul testifies that he had arrived in Jerusalem but twelve days before, having come neither to agitate nor to teach, but to worship. He challenges his opponents to present proof for their allegations. Since this is not in the cards, it is an effective demand. Paul follows suit by broadening his defense, resting it upon the doctrine of the resurrection. Let this be recognized as the issue and Paul is home free. Motivated by this hope, he had come to Jerusalem with alms and offerings for the temple. There he was found, purifying himself in accordance with cultic usage. So engaged, he was accused of desecration by Asian Jews, of whose absence he takes note. He soon returns to the subject of resurrection, and only the intervention of Felix prevents the delivery of a missionary appeal.

These two speeches are mirror images of one another. On every point Paul has triumphed, embarrassing his enemies and demonstrating the lack of competent witnesses to any relevant charges. The outlook is promising. When Lysias (whose position is known to us, but to neither Paul nor his accusers) appears, the case will be continued. After Felix relaxes the conditions of Paul's custody, it is clear that the tide has finally turned.

THE GOVERNOR AT HOME (24:23-27)

While waiting for Lysias to arrive, we are given a glimpse of private life. Felix and his wife Drusilla send for Paul and listen to his lectures. Life in the capital of a backward province can be dull, and the presence of learned teachers like Paul gave opportunity for diversion and cultural enrichment. This interlude demonstrates that Paul was welcome in the salons of high society and was received as a philosopher. Alas, however, Felix found the ethical rigors of Paul's system alarming and sought refuge in his packed agenda. Instruction was postponed, as was justice. Expenses being what they were, Felix was not loathe to receive a consideration. Since people of his position were unlikely to be obsessed with small bribes, it is clear that he thought Paul was well-to-do, as one might expect of a citizen of Rome and Tarsus. Paul is the leading example in Luke-Acts of a rich person who does not use his wealth for his own power or comfort. Instead he works. Felix, on the other hand, trails off down the path toward moral corruption. Alert readers might note that his wife was Jewish and speculate that the tentacles of conspiracy have slithered into the gubernatorial bedroom. So Paul must languish for two whole years, a victim now of maladministration. Throughout this section of Acts our hopes are raised and dashed again and again. Hope now must reside in the new governor, Porcius Festus.

A STUNNING DEVELOPMENT (25:1-12)

The dawn of a new administration brings the fresh air of integrity and efficiency. After no more than three days' rest from his arduous journey to the new station, the governor makes his way to Jerusalem. In a meeting with the priestly and other aristocracy, Festus learns about one of their enduring priorities: the case of Paul. They ask that he return Paul to Jerusalem. Behind the request lurks the old plan for an ambush. Festus, thankfully, does not fall for it. He invites the accusers to come to Caesarea and present whatever case they have. His doubts promise a speedy and fair trial.

A bit more than a week later they duly appear, for what looks like a replay of chap. 24. Paul denies any offense against the Jewish law, the temple, or Caesar. With the introduction of this crucial last word, he has begun to include in his defense a rebuttal of political charges. There is no information about the presence of witnesses. Nonetheless, the trial is over, and we await Festus's verdict. He fails us. "Wishing to do the Jews a favor," the proconsul proposes trial under him in Jerusalem. Although the place of trial was a matter of his own prerogative, he asks Paul's permission. Has bribery entered the picture? Festus's opaque request may be read in several ways. However it is understood, Paul is now in hot water, for the outcome of trips to Jerusalem is something about which he knows all too much. Implying that Festus wishes simply to hand him over to the Jews, he claims the right for trial before a Roman bench, closing with two dramatic Greek words: "I appeal to Caesar."

This is a stunning development. We had expected the simple answer no. Discomfited, Festus must find some way to regain control. An experienced bureaucrat, he elects to confer with his legal consultants to assess the ramifications of this demand. After a proper interval he emerges from the huddle and announces his decision in two crisp phrases: "You have appealed to Caesar; to Caesar you shall go." This has all the ring of a legal decision and redeems Festus from any appearance of confusion. Readers, however, have heard the voice of divine necessity in v. 10 ("ought") and recall 23:11 and 19:21. What looks like a legal can of worms tainted with the odor of corruption is the unfolding of God's plan.

TESTIMONY BEFORE A KING (25:13—26:32)

There matters rest, for Paul does not leave that day or the next. In the course of time a royal couple, Agrippa and Bernice, dropped in to pay their respects. Because their visit extended over several days, Festus had opportunity to lay before his guest the burden of this difficult case. Readers are privileged to hear their very words and witness Festus in action. He notes that the case is a hangover from his predecessor and goes on to report the meeting in Jerusalem, adding a very high-sounding statement of Roman legal principle, together with the new information that the leaders had demanded execution. (This, we know, is a falsehood.) Festus continued by noting his prompt calling of the case and gives his own impression of the matter. It is a purely theological dispute. (He must have nodded during the speech summarized in 25:7-8.) Festus did understand, however, that resurrection was the chief issue of debate. Utterly adrift on this sea of religious tempests, Festus claims, he attempted to soothe the waters with the perfectly innocent and reasonable proposal to let them have it out in Jerusalem (omitting at present the role he had proposed for himself in this procedure). The appeal dashed these hopes for a sensible settlement, and Paul is awaiting transmission to Rome. Agrippa finds all this quite interesting and allows that he would like to hear the fellow. The unreluctant Festus grants this request and sets an audience for the very next day.

In this way it came about that Paul's final defense of his life's work was set amid the splendor and pageantry provided by the visit of a Roman client king, joined on that occasion by the highest officers of the army and the elite of Caesarea. Festus opens the gala event with a brief background speech. In it we learn that the demand for Paul's death had been advanced by the assembled populace of Jerusalem (cf. Luke 23:18 for similar shouts in the case of Jesus, who also appeared before a petty monarch, 23:6-12). Notables like these realize how difficult such pressures are for officials to resist. Festus, following the hallowed footsteps of Pilate, finds his prisoner innocent, but notes that the appeal had rendered this opinion moot. The purpose of the present hearing is to provide the basis for an intelligent aide-mémoire to assist the imperial court. As a Jew, Agrippa will play a pivotal role in assessing the statement and serving the interests of justice. This is so convincing that even the most ardent admirer of Paul has difficulty in gaining enough distance to say, "If justice is your interest, Festus, release him."

Agrippa takes this overture as an invitation to assume the chair. With his permission Paul rises to address the distinguished throng, beginning with the gesture of a trained orator. What follows is the third account of his conversion, and one is tempted to skim it, but this is not advisable. His previous rendition had provided the story with a Semitic coloring. This edition is suitably Hellenic, but more than rhetorical flexibility is operative here. The three accounts of Paul's "conversion" show that it is an important vehicle for the message of Acts. The defense of Paul and his missionary heritage is a leading feature of this book. Each account has particular emphases. The first stressed, in a context of notable conversions, Paul's own change of allegiance. Through the successive presentations Luke has gradually transformed this story into a description of a prophetic call. (Note the allusions to the calls of Jeremiah [1:5-8], Ezekiel [2:1], and the servant [Isa. 42:7, 16] in vv. 16-18.) Both the opening and closing of Luke are recalled in this climactic oration. (To 26:18 compare Luke 1:17 and 2:32; to 26:23 compare Luke 24:46-47). Verses 16-17 bring Paul as close as possible to the circle of the apostles by the use of "appeared" (as in Easter appearances), "witness" (Luke 24:48), and "send" (the verb related to "apostle").

Paul here delivers his most important speech before his most distinguished audience. The King Agrippa scene is as close as we shall get to seeing a speech before the king at Rome.

The structure is autobiographical, setting forth Paul's Pharisaic background (4-8), his work as a persecutor, reversed by God's call (9-18), and his career as servant and witness (19-23). Despite its stress upon continuity in pursuit of the ancestral heritage, the speech reflects the ultimate separation of Judaism from Christianity. For Luke that is a sociological, not a theological, fact. Paul's story is a microcosm of Luke-Acts as a whole, beginning with devout Jews and ending in Rome with announcement of the fulfillment of the ancient promise.

This account dramatically contrasts the phases of Paul's life by intensifying his role as a persecutor. He sought to seize and kill all believers. The conversion is now a call. Both the blinding and Ananias episodes are omitted. The vocation comes from Jesus himself. It is the blind eyes of others that will be opened, not Paul's (v. 18). After a stirring summary of his labors to bring light to the nations (without stress upon gentiles), Paul moves to his climax, the resurrection of Jesus.

Festus intervenes, being the last to do so in Acts, with an objection that testifies to the magic of Paul's rhetoric and his own incapacity to grasp the subject. After a polite reply, Paul returns to his audience proper, Agrippa, who is better informed about these things, which are by no means the ravings of an isolated backwoods sect. Agrippa certainly does believe the prophets, does he not? Rather than pin the king, Paul answers for him. Suitably impressed by all this, Agrippa allows that Paul is not far from converting him. We are not sure how to take this utterance, but Paul erases any trace of an awkward moment with an elegantly phrased pious wish for the conversion of all. As usual, he has the last word, and with this hopeful prayer he offers his last words on the soil of the holy land. Through it Luke expresses his view of the tragic rejection of the message by Israel.

The king rises to leave, joined politely by the others. As they exit we catch their parting words affirming once more Paul's innocence. To the voices of the notables of Caesarea, Festus and

Agrippa add their own words. Their brief closing exchange is filled with regret for the necessity to pursue this unneeded appeal. Readers agree, but may take consolation in the favorable contents of the memorandum that will be forwarded. Whatever the outcome (for the capacity of Jews and pagans for manufacturing plots is not to be underestimated), there has been a favorable verdict by those best equipped to render it—a Jewish king and the Roman governor. This is the verdict that counts.

A vast amount of Acts has been concerned with Paul's legal predicament. Luke allots more verses to defense speeches by Paul than to his missionary sermons. One cannot say, however, that the quantity of material has untangled the legal situation. The witness of Paul as a prisoner who follows the way of Jesus is more important to Luke than his actual missionary work. In defending Paul, Luke was defending the church with which he was associated and in which he had been nurtured. The problems of Paul's relation to the Jerusalem church and his ultimate arrest there had raised questions about the legitimacy of his work. These are the questions Luke answers with his defense of Paul, faithful Jew and Christian.

A MODEL VOYAGE (27:1—28:10)

Acts 27:1 jars us with an abrupt leap, picking up the story from 25:25. Without preparation, the reader is thrust into narrative with a different tone and point of view. Return of the "we" heralds the latter. Our circle of vision is now much more restricted. The camera that could sweep through bedrooms and audience chambers of the procuratorial palace has been turned off. Reader and narrator are now enclosed within the circle of Paul, his companions, and, at times, their fellow voyagers. Acts has referred to numerous sea voyages. This is the instance selected for detailed examination and elaboration.

After all the hope and rising confidence expressed in the preceding chapter, the situation rudely reverts to a colder reality. Paul is one among other prisoners handed over to the charge of a centurion, Julius. Aristarchus, last heard of in Ephesus (19:29), and at least one other person accompany Paul. Their status is not clear. The trip begins as a coastal voyage along the shores of Syria and Asia Minor, familiar territory from earlier chapters. It also begins uneventfully, with no more to report than the routine details of daily movement. A bright note quickly appears when Julius reveals a humane character, granting Paul leave to be cared for by friends at Sidon. Paul's personality is having its normal effect. By excluding the "we" from these benefactions, the narrator makes it apparent that Paul is the only character of importance. At Myra the centurion secured passage on an Alexandrian grain ship bound for Italy. Now they are truly under way.

Progress from that point is disappointingly slow, however, due to contrary winds, and the vessel took refuge on the southern coast of Crete. The delay was costly, for October was advancing. At this point Paul dramatically intervenes with a prediction that the voyage if continued will bring loss of life, ship, and cargo. This advice went unheeded, for the harbor was inadequate. The advent of a favorable wind seemed to confirm the wisdom of finding better shelter in which to winter. So they put out with a confidence not shared by readers who have learned to respect Paul's views.

They should have done the same, for a savage northeaster came up, driving the ship before it. With considerable effort the trailing boat was brought inboard and additional lines to brace the vessel were secured in place. Fearing that the winds would drive them to disaster along the dangerous shoals off modern-day Libya, they lowered the mainsail and let the waves impel them. Those in charge of the voyage had lost all control over their fate. The next day they began to abandon their mission, jettisoning some cargo. Valuable gear followed in its wake two days later. At this point (vv. 17-20), the text separates the "we" from the crew. "They" have disregarded Paul and are paying the price.

After days without even sight of sun by day or stars by night, the company had reached the nadir of despair. They gave up, unable even to rouse themselves to take nourishment. At this last and lowest moment, Paul intervened. Despite the difficulties posed by the raging storm, he managed to gain the attention of the distracted passengers and cynical crew by rising to deliver a brief sermon. Opening with an "I told you so" to establish his credentials, Paul sets forth a message of hope based upon a vision reported in words intelligible to pagans. Divine necessity ("must," v. 24) will lead to the salvation of not only Paul but of all the ship's company. He will be the source of their deliverance. These words conclude with the practical observation that they must run upon an island.

After two weeks adrift between Greece and Sicily, signs of land appeared, confirmed by repeated soundings. The anchors were dropped to prevent running onto a reef in the dark. "They" prayed for day—and deliverance—to come. At this point the faithless crew sought to make off in the ship's boat. Paul, alert as ever, detected this desertion and advised the centurion. To prevent such an abandonment of helpless landlubbers, they set the boat adrift. This was a drastic measure, for now passengers and crew would have to make their way ashore without transport.

With the arrival of first light, Paul once more resumed the initiative, urging all to strengthen themselves with food for the work before them. He set a personal example, publicly offering thanks and breaking bread before eating. The others followed suit. At this point Luke notes the total complement of passengers and crew: 276. This is a "triangular" number (the sum of one through twenty-three) and thus invested with significance. This statistic indicates a transition: the darkness has passed and the storm is over.

Full light revealed an unknown bay with a beach. The water was too shallow for them to run upon the beach, and they hit a shoal. Waves soon began to break up the vessel. The soldiers thought it best to kill the prisoners lest they escape, but Julius refused, determined as he was to rescue Paul. This is the last plot the hero of Acts will elude. Roman intervention has saved him again. By one means or another all get themselves ashore, fulfilling Paul's promise.

Local "barbarians" informed the shipwrecked band that the island was Malta. Because inhabitants of coastal regions regularly supplemented their incomes with the windfalls provided by shipwrecks and were not always above eliminating or enslaving any survivors, their kind reception of this bedraggled and freezing company was little short of a miracle. They quickly ignited a fire to overcome the effects of the sea and the chilling rain. Not one to remain inactive, Paul occupied himself with gathering driftwood for the blaze. While so engaged he attracted a viper, which fastened itself to his hand to escape the heat. Observing this venomous creature affixed to the refugee, the superstitious natives were moved to meditate upon the ways of "providence." Clearly the prisoner was a murderer whom the god would not allow to elude his appointed fate. Justice will out. When, on the contrary, he shrugged this irritant into the blaze with no signs of snakebite, they leapt to the opposite conclusion and enrolled him among the gods. Despite the inadequacy of their religious categories, we here catch a glimpse of the nimbus of the divine that encompassed Paul even amid adversity.

Barbarian ministrations soon gave way to more suitable entertainment provided by the hospitable local ruler. In return for Publius's generosity, Paul visited and cured his afflicted father. News of this spread and led to the opportunity for Paul to distinguish himself by healing local invalids. So the beneficiaries became benefactors and were properly honored with material and other rewards.

Luke has devoted fifty-four verses to the story of the voyage and its aftermath. Good and famous as this tale is, one has to wonder why so much space has been allotted to this adventure. In the first place, appearances do not deceive. From the earliest days of recorded literature, the fascination of adventure at sea has held a high place in stories of entertainment. This is Luke's contribution to that tradition. We are meant to enjoy it.

Acts 27:1—28:10 exhibits Paul in a variety of heroic aspects and roles. He envisions the folly of going ahead after the season for navigation is past. When all seems lost he remains calm and offers the promise of deliverance, comforting even tough sailors. Paul stifles an incipient mutiny through his vigilance and convinces the entire party to strengthen themselves with sustenance. On land he sloughs off the bite of a viper and places the whole company in his debt by dispensing his healing gifts. After years in prison, Paul shows that he is still a natural leader and master of all that he surveys.

This voyage, with its many dangers—shipwreck in Africa, sinking in a storm, death by starvation and shock, running aground at night, abandonment by the crew, shoaling, murder, drowning, reception by unfriendly natives, and exposure to the elements—demonstrates most convincingly that amid all the apparent storms and caprices of

fate, God is the one in charge. Even the elements bow before the
agents of the Almighty (28:10; cf. Luke 8:22-25). The core of the
plan is the requirement that Paul testify at Rome, come hell or high
water. Both came, without avail. (The symbol for hell is the serpent,
Satan's most famous disguise.) In conformity with biblical and other
ancient traditions, Luke used the sea-voyage and wreck as a symbol
for the workings of justice and fate, and the proper response to
danger and imminent death. This imagery was so ingrained in an-
tiquity that readers would expect a shipwreck story to present an
underlying message.

These episodes occupy the structural place in Acts held by the
passion and resurrection in Luke (23–24). Those who read into
Peter's experience in chap. 12 a symbolic death and resurrection
will find here a more lengthy parallel in the experience of Paul.
Prison and shipwreck were two common ancient metaphors for
death. Luke knew of the deaths of both Peter and Paul. By presenting
these martyrdoms in symbolic form, he was able to suggest their
ultimate victory over the grave through the resurrection of Jesus. A
number of specific allusions enhance this interpretation, including
the contrast between night (death) and day (resurrection), the dis-
appearance of sun and stars (as at Jesus' crucifixion, Luke 23:44-
45), allusions to the story of Jonah (as in 27:19), whose adventures
were read as a foreshadowing of Jesus (as suggested by "the third
day," v. 19), and the presence of a friendly centurion (Luke 23:47).
The meal scene in 27:33-35 corresponds to the recognition at Emmaus (Luke 24:30-31). Acts 28:1-6 has features of the Easter appearances. Paul is a kind of divine, indestructible being, delivered
from the tomb of the sea. His death was inappropriately expected
(cf. Luke 24:5: "Why do you seek the living among the dead?").
For a proper understanding of Acts it should be noted that these
"parallels" to Jesus' passion and resurrection occur in two famous
tales, one marked by humor and drama, the other by great adventure.
The medium for Luke's story is good stories.

Another level of interpretation looks to the central Lukan image
of the "journey." "The Way" is his preferred name for Christianity.
Luke presents the teachings of Jesus in the context of his journey
toward Jerusalem. The second half of Acts is dominated by the

famous journeys of Paul. Luke exploits these movements as metaphors of and models for the journey undertaken by each believer. Jesus teaches the wisdom needed to survive the curse. Paul illustrates its excitement. As he approaches the end of his work, Luke uses this final journey to show the faith required for safe conclusion of the voyage through the dangers and tempests of life.

The universal application of this symbolism is accomplished by the presence of a sacramental dimension. As Peter's passion in chap. 12 made use of initiatory symbols, so Acts 27 evokes Baptism by immersion in the depths and death, followed by rising to new life victorious over death. (Again, note the viper. The eucharistic symbolism is quite apparent in 27:33-35.) By these means Luke sets forth the victory of the Christian cult over the powers of Satan and the forces of paganism.

In this climactic story the Christian faith and community come into their own as benefactor to the Roman Empire. Luke saw the church as a means for affirming what was good in Roman life and as an instrument for enhancing, rather than condemning, the process and progress of civilization. Ancient leaders shared with their gods the titles of "savior" and "benefactor." Repeated references to "salvation" (variously rendered by RSV) point to the locus of true rescue. Successful encounter with "barbarians" evinces the civilizing power of the faith. Paul works miracles in 27:1—28:10, but not in connection with mission. He is a benefactor to the pagans aboard the ship, Publius, and other Maltese people.

In accordance with its parallel place to the death and resurrection of Jesus, Paul's rescue is his ultimate vindication by a heavenly court. This carries rather more weight than the opinions of any earthly tribunal. Having heard the views of Festus and Agrippa, we now see the viewpoint of the Almighty. The encounter with the viper is once more the apex of this representation. A further evidence of this vindication is that Paul on Malta does not appear to be a prisoner and remains free until he reports to Rome.

By this cataclysm Christianity is shorn from its Jewish parent. Acts 27:1—28:10 takes place in a pagan world. When Jews reappear in Rome, it will be the same old story, told again only to confirm the separation. Within this pagan world continuity is maintained, for Paul carries on the ministry of Jesus (compare Acts 28:7-10 to Luke 4:38-41). The close of Paul's ministry reiterates the beginning of his master's ministry.

WE COME TO ROME (28:11-31)

When the end of winter brings a resumption of the journey, the "we" embraces only Paul and his companions. Julius, his soldiers, and the other passengers are no longer with us. Paul is now master of his time. The entrance to Rome resembles the entry into Jerusalem. In both cases the arrival gains two mentions, for emphasis (21:15-17; 28:14-16). A two-week delay at Puteoli proved opportune, allowing the Christians at Rome to send a delegation to prepare a triumphant welcome for the arriving V.I.P. This escort and acclamation is the only role they play in Acts.

Only after the grand entry does Paul revert to the status of prisoner, although the permission to live in quarters of his choice with a single guard softens this blow. Paul received, or assumed, permission to invite the leading Jews of Rome to his lodgings. They were not loathe to visit the accused, who offered them a brief but eloquent defense of his position. The speech opens and closes with affirmations of his loyalty to the faith. (His circumstances closely resemble those of Jesus, who also had been seized by the Jews and delivered to the Romans, who would gladly have freed him had it not been for the objections of the former.) Appeal was his only refuge, but he has no case against his own. The listeners hear him politely and assure him that no Jewish slander against him has penetrated to Rome. They have, however, heard much negative about "this sect." Paul will be an apologist for it. Therefore a date was set for his presentation. A large crowd came to his (obviously roomy) abode. From daybreak to dusk Paul expounded the Scriptures to prove that they spoke of Jesus. As usual, some found this convincing while others doubted. When the meeting breaks up on this discordant note, Paul gives his final last word, a quote from Isaiah, "to *your* fathers" (v. 25). For the third time Paul solemnly announces the shift to the gentiles. The Jews have struck out.

Acts contains three lengthy Scripture quotes: by Peter, in the beginning (Joel), James, in the middle (Amos), and Paul, at the end (Isaiah). These strategically placed citations proclaim the promise of the Spirit to all, the inclusion of gentiles, and the rejection of hardhearted Jews. Each is placed on the lips of a major character. The sequence illustrates the succession of leadership in the early church.

A brief sequel follows this closing announcement. For two years Paul received all comers and proclaimed his message, without loss of courage or prohibition from the outside. Through numerous subtle details Luke has bound the conclusion of his work to its beginning, as well as to the opening and closing of Acts. The "hope of Israel" proclaimed in v. 20 is the same hope that motivated Simeon and Anna and gave disappointment to the travelers to Emmaus (Luke 2:25-28; 24:21). Jesus' first sermon also made use of a long quote from Isaiah. That sermon presaged both the gentile mission and his rejection (Luke 4:16-30). One of its themes was sight for the blind. Paul's final message speaks of blindness for the sighted. Thus the story moves from the promises announced as fulfilled by Jesus to the rejection of them encountered by Paul. Acts 28:28 completes the circle, with its reference to "the salvation of God," harking back to the words used to introduce the forerunner (Luke 3:5-6). The final verse of Acts 28 echoes 1:1-3 and has a structure similar to Luke 24:52-53.

By these devices Luke has done more than provide his opus with a fine structural frame wrapped in an artistic ribbon. Through them speaks his claim of the essential continuity of the message revealed throughout the history of salvation, a continuity brought into doubt by the refusal of most Jews to accept it. Acts closes with the assurance that Paul is an authentic witness to the message.

The Jews will no longer be primary targets. Individual Jews will continue to convert, but the mission to the synagogue is over. Believers will affiliate with Christian communities composed of gentiles and right-thinking Jews rather than linger about the synagogue. The "ends of the earth" have been reached with the closing of the synagogue door after many attempts at admittance and the opening

of that enormous door to the gentiles. The story ends in the imperial
capital. Christians will find their earthly lodgings within this realm.

CONCLUSION

So concludes the tale that began in Judea with an aging, childless
couple devoid of personal and national hope, and finishes in the
throbbing heart of the world with bold and unhindered proclamation
of the kingdom. The scope of Luke's canvas and the grandeur of
his execution enhance but do not mask the simplicity and clarity of
his message. The chasm between Rome and Judea, Jerusalem and
Athens, has been closed through the ministries of Jesus and Paul.
Luke's resolution of the questions raised by this transition has been
so successful that it has become *the* story of Christian origins.

This is to say that the end of Acts, like that of any good book,
provides not only resolution and closure but also openness and
mission. The "scene" depicted in 28:28 has no ending. It is a
program for the future, not a comment upon the past. Luke's own
last word is a perfect summary of his writings, a one-word closure
that is, at the same time, an opening, a bright and invigorating bid
to the future, an assurance that "the ends of the earth" is not the
arrival at a boundary, but realization of the limitless promises of the
dominion of God.